DOWNLOAD YOUR FREE CHECKLIST NOW!

If you've ever checked out an equine supply website or stopped by a tack shop, you might find your head swimming regarding all of the stuff people buy to help them care for their horses. How do you decide what you need to buy? I've created this checklist to help new horse owners get organized right from the start.

Go to **https://free.meredithhillbook.com/checklist** or
scan this code

to download it for free

HELP!
I BOUGHT A NEW
HORSE!

What First Time Horse Owners Need to Know About
Grooming, Riding, Training, and Horse Care

MEREDITH HILL

ISBN: 978-1-953714-53-4

Introductory Horse Care for Beginners

Before Your Horse Comes Home

Meredith Hill

CONTENTS

INTRODUCTION

When I was a child, I had plenty of toys including puzzles, games, and dolls. I had coloring books galore, and my parents even shelled out the extra cash for the good crayons. My bed was covered by a whole zoo of stuffed animals, but none of these playthings delighted me as much as my herd of toy horses.

From a young age, I was drawn to horses. No one really knows why. I don't come from a long line of professional equestrians. In fact, my parents find the large, smelly beasts just a few steps away from completely abhorrent. We didn't live near a horse farm, or in a super "horsey" part of the country. My entire experience with horses was limited to pony rides at fairs and festivals that rolled through town from time to time. And yet, I was completely obsessed with anything horse-related.

As soon as I learned how to read, my favorite subject was -- you guessed it -- horses. Sure, I loved reading those highly fictional books in which a lonely girl walks past a field and magically becomes friends with an untamable horse. However,I found those tales highly suspicious. You see, even at a young age, I was devouring horse care books feverishly-- sometimes reading two or three at a time to make sure I was getting all the facts and concepts right.

I suppose I thought, in my child's mind, that if I proved myself knowledgeable, my parents would miraculously decide that I was ready to have a horse. I even demonstrated my skill and proficiency in horse care by creating a "stall" right by the door in the corner of our garage, so my "steed" would have easy access to turnout in the backyard. Granted, the "stall" was childishly constructed out of sawhorses and boards tied together with some yarn spirited from my craft supplies. All I did was make it incredibly difficult to walk through the garage. But before my parents made me take everything down, I used this demonstration as my dissertation on why I should be permitted to get a pony.

I explained how the adequately sized pony for me would be twelve to thirteen hands high, which wasn't that much bigger than our riding lawn mower. Plus, if we fenced in the entire backyard, we'd have the proper amount of forage for my beast. I could ride it up and down the block, just like I did with my bike. It made perfect sense to me!

To their credit, my parents let me down easy with explanations of things like zoning laws. They asked me what we would do with all of the manure my pony would produce, and after poking many valid holes in my hypothetical barn set up, they returned to praying for this phase of childhood obsession to end.

Except it didn't.

When I was seven, we moved to a new town. Our subdivision was still being slowly constructed, with dirt mounds and empty lots surrounding our new home. As an only child in a new school district, in a neighborhood that hadn't yet been constructed, I was desperately lacking interaction with children my own age. In hopes that I would meet some other children and realize horses were too much work, my parents finally relented and signed me up for horseback riding lessons

In retrospect, I'm absolutely certain the barn owner thought I was some twerpy, know-it-all kid when I showed up for my first lesson. Smartly dressed in Dockers and a jean jacket (it was the 1980s, after all), I borrowed an ancient helmet from the lesson stock and was thrilled at my first opportunity to actually experience all of the things

I'd been reading about. I finally got to touch and hold and use all of the tools I'd read about. This was the curry comb, and it is used in a circular motion to scrub off dirt and dead skin. This was the body brush, which is used to flick off all of the grit the curry comb pulled up. This was the hoof, and that spongy part in the middle was called the frog. "You don't wanna poke that with the hoof pick," I cleverly informed the professional instructor who was trying his best to show me what to do.

I'm sure my enthusiasm was overwhelming, bordering on obnoxious, but in that moment, my dearest dream was finally coming true. I threw my little leg, clad in slacks, over the stalwart lesson pony for the first time on a crisp September morning in 1987. Even today, thirty-four years later, I still remember the amazing sense of belonging I felt during that first lesson.

Surely, it was just a matter of time before my parents gave in to my obsession, right? Sadly, no. Despite my obvious delight, my parents continued to hope that I would find something less smelly, frightening, and expensive to appreciate. I campaigned heavily for a horse of my own, but it was in vain. Instead, I fed my obsession the best I could by reading every book I could find, watching television programs and films, subscribing to magazines, and trying my hardest to eke out all the extra barn time I could before and after my weekly barn visit.

Once I reached my teenage years, I was permitted to work at farms in exchange for lessons. I cleaned stalls and pastures from six to noon. I painted fences, stacked bales of hay, polished tack, sorted equipment, and most importantly, I learned. I learned the difference between various types of feed. I felt and smelled a variety of hays. I built muscles and calluses picking out stalls, but I gained impressive insight into manure management and parasite control. I got first-hand experience deworming horses, changing bandages, and learning what to look for when it came to common equine ailments. I came home sweaty, exhausted, and covered in grit, but I can honestly say those were some of the happiest days of my teenage years.

So when did I finally get my own horse? I was twenty, in college, and an active member of the intercollegiate equestrian team. My favorite lesson horse, a large and ancient Thoroughbred, came up for sale, and in the true spirit of those "misfit girl and horse" books I'd read as a child, I bought him. This was an incredibly unwise investment for someone in their senior year of college, but I refused to have it any other way. I headed to the barn after class or my work-study program and worked long past midnight, trying to complete enough chores to pay off my board. While my classmates went on extravagant trips during the holiday breaks, I toiled in the barn.

The summer after graduation, my long-awaited dream horse contracted equine protozoal myeloencephalitis. EPM is a neurological disease contracted through exposure to opossum feces. A highly experimental and extremely expensive treatment was offered, and despite being a broke college student, I took the chance to help my buddy feel better. I watched my horse suffer from loss of balance and pain so extreme that he would just lean against the walls of his stalls. He made a partial recovery, but upon his vet's recommendation and with the help of his previous owner, we found him a very nice retirement home. My time with my first horse was short, but he lived a long, happy life in his retirement home, and I went on to become heavily involved in horse rescue and rehabilitation.

So why did I tell you this lengthy and somewhat depressing tale? There are actually many reasons for sharing this story. First, because any time can be the right time to bring your first horse into your life. There seems to be a strange notion that, if you were not exposed to horses as a child, you can't possibly become involved in horse ownership as an adult. This is absolutely false, as being an adult with a steady income is probably the best time to take on the responsibility!

Additionally, I want to stress the importance of being a knowledgeable horse owner. Horses are extremely delicate. They are one of few species of animals who can actually die due to indigestion. Their digestive tract includes nearly 100 feet of miraculously suspended intestine, which is balanced precariously on long, fragile limbs that end in a single toe. Their fine-tuned flight instincts as prey animals can turn plastic grocery bags into monsters and shadows into deep pits of despair.

The idea that you can buy a horse and throw it in a field to take care of itself is an incredibly dangerous misconception. If you are not prepared to provide the high level care these amazing animals require, you may wish to consider leasing a horse instead of buying one. In this arrangement, you'll enjoy access to a horse without having to worry about the complicated care.

If my story didn't deter you and you're excited about cleaning stalls before the roosters wake up, soaking an abscessed hoof on hot summer days, and willing to walk acres of field to retrieve a lost horse shoe, then horse care is for you.

Do you have to study this book and others like it obsessively like I did? No, but it helps. The art of keeping horses alive and thriving is constantly changing, as science reveals more and more information that updates the old farmer's way. There are plenty of time-tested approaches to horse care that work beautifully, but there are also some modern approaches that make things a little easier for horse and human alike. As a horse owner, you will constantly be learning about your horse and its needs. Putting as much knowledge into your mental encyclopedia as you can will help you troubleshoot the infinite number of challenges you will experience as a horse owner, from a broken fence line, to dealing with pests and insects, to understanding what it means when your horse is acting "not quite right," or NQR, in vet terms.

Horses have special requirements to keep them happy from day to day, and unfortunately, horse care doesn't get as much exposure as the care of more common companions, like dogs or cats. There is far more to keeping a horse alive than giving it grass and water.

Therefore, I wanted to create a comprehensive guide for the first-time horse owner, to help them be exceptionally prepared to add a horse into their life.

I always recommend working with a professional, especially if you don't have any personal horse experience. Take lessons. Join 4-H or the Pony Club. Volunteer at a local barn. Read books, scientific studies, magazines, and articles on the topic.

Coincidentally, I caution you to not rely on opinion-based anecdotes you read on the internet for your equine knowledge. While there are many great resources out there, some of which I've included at the end of this book to get you started, there is a great deal of misinformation to be found on the internet. As mentioned before, horses are extremely delicate, and a simple mistake can easily end a horse's life. I say this not to scare you, but to emphasize how important it is to gather as much high-quality knowledge as you can before you bring your first horse home.

In the following pages, you'll learn all of the ins and outs of horse care. We'll take a look at everything a horse needs to stay well. We'll evaluate whether a home barn is best for you or if you would be better off boarding at a facility by weighing the pros and cons of each option. From pest management to where to put all of that manure, we'll take a look at all of the need-to-knows for taking care of your own horse. We'll also look at what goes into a feeding program, along with supplements and parasite control. You'll learn what to look for in a vet and a farrier and when to call them. And of course, we'll look at all of the supplies and equipment necessary to be ready for your horse's homecoming.

Horse care is extremely rewarding. Through the sweat and grit come the tears and the triumph. Today, with two horses of my own, I'm still the same "horse-crazy" kid I've always been. My calluses have calluses, and I'd probably drive a much nicer car if I didn't have horses, but none of that matters to me when I hear my giant fluff balls nicker for me when I walk in the barn door.

Is horse care a lot of work? More than you can imagine. Is it worth it? I wouldn't have it any other way.

SECTION 1: SETTING EXPECTATIONS

For those who are new to horse ownership, there may have been several terms in the introduction that were unfamiliar, or raised questions. How many types of hay are there? What do you mean by "parasite control?" Does having horses mean I need to exterminate every opossum I find?

Horse care can be very complicated, especially when you're diving into the concept for the first time. Much like people, different horses need different types of care. There is no "one-size-fits-all" universal standard for horse care. Over time, you may need to tinker with your program to ensure that the needs of your horse are being met. Things like overall health, the quality and quantity of natural forage, and the level of activity your horse performs on a daily basis can require you to rethink everything, from the type of feed you use to how much bedding you put in your horse's stall.

External factors can impact your horse care regimen as well. You'll find yourself paying close attention to the weather forecast, for example. Horses generally don't mind getting wet, but lightning and metal horse shoes don't mix well. Further, too much mud can lead to hoof issues. When it's hot, your horse might be at a greater risk for overheating and potential colic, and when the temperatures plummet, water buckets freeze and your equine buddy may need extra nutrition to help him cope with the cold.

It may seem a bit obvious, but in order to really appreciate what goes into horse care, you need to understand a thing or two about horses. Anyone who has enjoyed the companionship of a horse could write a book called "Everything I Know about Horses," and no two books would be identical. In fact, each book would contain so many contradictions, exceptions, footnotes, and addendums that no one could possibly get through it without a massive headache.

So instead, this section is going to overview the partnership we enjoy with horses in a manner that highlights some of the most important things about horse care that aren't as patently obvious as others. There are many assumptions and generalizations about horses in the world that simply aren't true or are even potentially dangerous when applied universally. In this section, I'll endeavor to reveal some common misconceptions and "I didn't know that" moments I've shared with many first-time owners and caretakers. While we'll examine some of the very basics, I want to empower readers to understand their individual horse and not just the general concept of "a horse." What *your* horse needs may be very different from what your best friend's horse needs.

It's my opinion-- and that of many professionals in the equine world-- that the more you know the beast, the more prepared you are to realize you don't know everything about them. As paradoxical as that sounds, you should start to understand what that statement means as you read on.

In the following chapters, we'll look at the basics of what makes horses tick and how our relationship with them works. While I wish there were a universal handbook, I think the only generalization we can make about horses is "all horses are unique." As you gain more experience with them, you'll understand exactly how true that statement is.

Chapter 1: Familiarizing Yourself with Horses

When you stop and think about it, it's really a bad idea to tangle with horses. Horses are large, quadrupedal prey animals. They're much larger than we are, both in height and weight. They're very muscular and, when motivated, incredibly fast, but they're just as prepared for fight as they are for flight. Their hooves are quite dense, and any of the four can strike out and kick to keep threats at bay. They have large teeth that continually grind the tough fibers of hay, grass, and grain to a digestible pulp. If the horse feels the need to protect itself, those same teeth can gnash through flesh very easily. Horses are big, fast, and dangerous, and it's important to keep this in mind at all times.

Horses are also among the most sensitive and empathetic animals humans have domesticated. As prey animals, they're naturally tuned in to their surroundings at all times. Their wide set eyes pick up all the motion around them, and their large ears swivel around to catch every nuance of sound in a 360-degree radius. Your horse will grow to understand patterns in how you move, how you speak, and how you interact with them. The short, hard strokes of the curry comb on their backs during a regular grooming session will tell them all about the bad day you had. The way your voice cracks when you call their name will expose how sad you've been feeling. Your super-relaxed demeanor will clue them in when you're having a good day. You can't keep secrets from a horse.

Likewise, as many wise horse experts have intoned, "horses don't lie." They have bad moods. Sometimes they don't feel good. Sometimes they flat out don't want to do whatever it is that you, as the human, have decided you need to be doing right now. Even more often, they simply don't understand what the human is asking of them.

Imagine, if you will, that you're hanging out in your bedroom. All of a sudden, someone walks in, makes you turn off your music and get out of bed. You have to put down the snack you were enjoying. They tie you up in the hallway, throw a backpack on you, and make you go for a hike.

Some of you might think, "Are you kidding? I love hikes! Let's do this!" Others are thinking, "Drop my snack and get out of bed? I don't think so!" Horses have the same variety of attitudes as we do. Some really enjoy working, and others need a little coaxing to get them prepared for the task ahead of them. Just as some mornings you wake up on the wrong side of the bed, so can your horse. They are not machines. They have bad days too. They are living beings who are doing the best they can with what they've got, just like you and me.

Just like people, horses also come in different shapes and sizes. The unit of measurement used to indicate how tall a horse is is called a "hand." A hand equals four inches. According to horse folklore, four inches is approximately the width of a man's hand from thumb to the outside of the pinkie finger. In the days before standard measurements, people would quite literally measure horses with their hands. Despite the development of more accurate measurements, the tradition of using the term "hands" when describing a horse's height remains. Therefore, if someone says a horse is 15 hands high, the horse is 60 inches tall.

Bear in mind, horses aren't measured from the ground to the top of their head. Any horse can raise or lower his head, which would change their measurements every time they bent down to graze. The top of their hip isn't used either since building muscle can cause a horse's hindquarters to grow in size. Instead, a horse's height is measured from the ground to the top of their withers. The withers are the spot where a horse's neck meets its back. For most horses, this is the tallest point of their body at all given times. There are exceptions, as some breeds tend to have hindquarters that tower above their withers, and spinal conditions such as lordosis can create a rather twisted version of a sway-backed horse. The distance from the withers to the ground very rarely changes, even as muscles grow or deteriorate, which is why this is used as the point of measurement for all horses' height.

To be considered a horse, the equine must measure over 14.2 hands (58 inches or 1.47 meters). Anything under this height is considered a pony. You may hear owners of giant 18 hand horses referring to their beasts as "my pony," but bear in mind this is more of a colloquial term of endearment, kind of like calling your grown cat a kitty.

In fact, there are many terms that horse people use to identify their beast. A mare is an adult female horse. A female horse under the age of four years is referred to as a filly. A male horse under the age of four years is a colt. An intact adult male horse is a stallion, while an adult male horse who has been castrated is a gelding. All of these terms may have different colloquial definitions, which muddies the water of understanding. For example, a mare with a feisty personality may be known to her humans as a "filly" for her entire life, though that's not technically accurate. This is similar to a parent calling her adult daughter "my little girl" despite her advanced age.

There are approximately 400 different horse breeds in the world today, though equine geneticists and breeders will argue the exact number eternally. Nearly every horse breed was created by crossing various bloodlines, which begs the question: "What was the original horse?" Thoroughbreds, for example, are alleged to have descended from three Foundation Arabian sires. The American Mustang tracks its bloodlines to the runaway horses of Spanish explorers. The American Quarter Horse is the result of crossing the horses of Spanish settlers with those of the English settlers. The Morgan horse breed is descended from a single stallion named Figure, who's own pedigree included a dash of Arabian, a sprinkle of Thoroughbred, and more than a little Welsh Cob, according to popular consensus.

Today, breeds are frequently evolving. The Georgian Grand, for example, is a rather recently acknowledged breed achieved by pairing a Friesian horse with an American Saddlebred. Another more modern breed is the American Sugarbush Harlequin Draft Horse, which was very carefully and deliberately bred from a particular Percheron bloodline paired with warmblood/Appaloosa crosses.

While some breed purists refuse to acknowledge some of the more modern breeds, or prefer to call them "crosses," there's no denying that certain breed attributes can contribute to the overall care needs of a particular horse. For example, Thoroughbreds can be what we call "hard keepers," in that they will lose weight whenever they're stressed, cold, or bored. Miniature ponies can be at high risk for medical conditions that come about from overfeeding. Appaloosas often have vision issues, and Quarter Horses from particular bloodlines can inherit genetic muscular problems, including HYPP, which can cause tremors and paralysis.

Additionally, some horses are better at certain jobs than others due to their breeding and conformation. Thoroughbreds that are bred for racing tend to be tall, lean, bold, and athletic. This makes them ideal for speed-based competition throughout their lives, whether that means pole bending or three-day eventing. Draft horses have the size and musculature to pull heavy loads, which makes them invaluable for pulling carriages or farm work.

Then there are gaited horses. Nearly every horse can walk, trot, and canter, which are the three main gaits of the typical riding horse. Some horses have extra manners of movement. The Paso Fino has quick-stepping gaits that make it appear to glide. Icelandic horses, though small in stature, seem to soar across the ground when they tolt. Standardbreds can pace very quickly on the racetrack, allowing them to cover a full mile in less than two minutes. Tennessee Walkers, Saddlebreds, and Missouri Fox Trotters are all examples of horses who have their own unique set of gaits.

So how do all of these differences translate to their care? To begin with, the amount of living space required. Not only will a bigger horse need a taller roof over its head, but it will need a larger space to stretch its legs as well. A horse bred to be very active will likely be less content with roaming around a field or standing in a stall and will need plenty of exercise. Gaited horses may require special shoes or hoof care to accommodate the different wear patterns they have from moving in a unique way. Some horses will need a lot of food to match their genetically predisposed metabolism while others are what we call "air ferns," meaning it seems as though they could gain weight just by breathing.

I have personally enjoyed the companionship of two very tall, very lean Thoroughbred geldings, a pregnant pony mare of unknown origins, a Quarter Horse mare with impeccable breeding, an aged Appaloosa gelding, and a very expressive Tennessee Walking Horse gelding. If I listed the care instructions for each one, you might think I was talking about six different species, rather than six wonderful horses. I have cared for horses who have multiple pages of care instructions just to get that single horse through the day. Some of this is based on owner preference and the job the horse is currently doing, but a great deal of their needs are determined by health, genetics, weather, and activity level, just like any other living creature.

Therefore, it is the responsibility of each horse owner to understand their horse on a nearly cellular level. There's a popular saying: "You don't ride bloodlines." You do, however, need to care for your horse based on its size, shape, breed, and even bloodlines.

The topic of various breeds and breeding is absolutely fascinating, and I recommend taking some time to do some research on the topic, especially if you're shopping for a horse that can do a very particular job. There are several links in the "Resources" section that can guide you to further information on this topic, so take some time to really explore the widely diverse world of *Equus caballus*.

Knowing more about horses can help you appreciate their behavior, moods, and care needs on a deeper level. As a horse owner, you'll quickly realize that you can never learn too much about these amazing animals and their quirks.

Chapter 2: The Many Considerations of Horse Ownership

Every day of horse ownership is new and different. One day, your horse might be super cuddly and almost make itself a nuisance begging for attention. The next day, it might be content with food, water, and being left alone. Living with a horse is like living with another human, in the way that you don't know what you're in for when you wake up in the morning. You just have to find a way to coexist.

It may sound like having a horse in your life is incredibly difficult physically, emotionally, and monetarily, but there are plenty of benefits to sharing your life with your horse.

Granted, most people no longer require horses for transportation, though there are still plenty of areas in which horses, mules, and donkeys are still very much valued for their ability to pull a cart, haul a rider around, or carry a heavy load. In many areas, horses provide vital contributions to agriculture by pulling plows in territories difficult for machines to navigate, or by dragging wagons for long distances. Horses are able to carry up to 20% of their body weight on their back. A horse can also pull up to 10% of its body weight in dead weight, though when wheels are added, a horse can pull up to 1.5 times its own body weight. A pair or a team of horses can pull tremendous loads reaching up to thousands of pounds. Horses are strong, nimble, sure-footed, and can navigate steep, muddy, and rocky terrain with admirable speed and endurance.

All of these qualities-- and more-- are what make riding, driving, and in-hand interacting with horses so delightful. There are many different disciplines, or styles, of riding which open the door to many ways in which you can work with your horse. Some people choose to study one particular discipline for their entire equine career, while others (myself included) prefer to explore as many as possible.

Riding, driving, and showmanship don't have to be all about horse shows and competition, either. There are plenty of equestrians who enjoy trail riding in their spare time, or practice dressage just for fun. One of the most common misconceptions about being an equestrian is that you need to spend loads of money to trailer your horse around to various big-name competitions to win points and prizes. Sure, horse shows can be a lot of fun, but they can also be very stressful for you and your horse. Once you've taken lessons for a while and have established a solid foundation in the discipline of your choice, you may wish to talk to your instructor about showing. But in the meantime, as long as you and your horse are having a good time, you don't need to have serious competitions or even a long term goal in mind.

Therefore, while some equestrians would say that the primary benefit of their horse is its ability to help them get work done, others would say the best thing about their horse is the fun they have together.

Furthermore, horses can be great companions. Their highly-tuned instincts make them incredibly perceptive of the nuances in your behaviors and moods. Nearly every horse owner has lost count of how many times they've broken down and cried on their horse's shoulder, or treated their horse like a therapist and told them absolutely everything that's going on in their life and in their heart. They are very good listeners and can usually be encouraged to listen to you as long as you need them to. However, you might just have to bribe them a little with scritchy-scratches on their favorite itchy spot, or a handful of treats.

Author's Anecdote: Old Mare's Tales about Mean Horses

We've all heard the old tales about some distant relative or friend's horse who was "nasty as could be" or "bit everyone he ever met", but that's actually pretty uncommon in the horse world. Yes, there are mean horses, but in many cases, their attitudes correlate to poor treatment, lack of training, or physical pain.

After nearly a decade in horse rescue, I have only ever encountered one horse who was "nasty as could be". She was a gorgeous little filly who had been surrendered by her breeder after being weaned because she kicked him with enough ferocity to break his leg. We worked with her slowly, grooming her, teaching her to lead, and growing her accustomed to having people near her. She was very smart and learned quickly, but her temper would come out of nowhere.

Horses typically prefer "flight" over "fight" and provide many visual cues with their body language to indicate when they're upset. They'll pin their ears, raise their head, swish their tail, bare their teeth, or tuck their hindquarters to indicate they're upset. This particular horse did none of these, which is how she ended up sending several seasoned equine professionals to the emergency room.

A thorough medical exam uncovered evidence of traumatic brain injury. Whether she experienced an accident careening around as a baby, or in the womb, we'll never know. But knowing that there was a physical cause for her attitude helped us adjust our care routine to help her become more comfortable, and kept us safer.

While horses can have bad days and foul moods, if you notice an abrupt or lingering change in temperament in your horse, consider whether physical pain might be the source of their attitude shift. Anything from an abscess in the hoof to a saddle pinching their back the wrong way can cause a horse to become grumpy, moody, or short-tempered. It's always a good idea to have your vet come out to evaluate your equine friend when things don't seem as they should be.

Sharing your time with a horse isn't just great for your mental health. It can be highly beneficial for your physical health as well. Horseback riding is one of the few activities in which your body is constantly exercising every muscle at once. Much like yoga, you'll need to learn to relax, stretch, flex, and move various parts of your body simultaneously While many non-equestrians will argue that riding is just a matter of sitting on a horse's back while they do all the work, the aching abductors, abdominals, and oblique muscles of any rider who has recently worked on sitting trot will beg to differ.

Even if you don't ride your horse, caring for a horse is still very physically demanding work. A bale of hay can weigh between 50 and 75 pounds. A bag of feed is typically 50 pounds. Water buckets must be dumped and refilled, and manure must be removed, with fresh bedding replaced daily. Moreover, horses ought to be groomed frequently to maintain a healthy coat, which requires vigorous motion in the arms and shoulders. Picking dirt and debris out of a horse's hooves requires bending over and asking the horse to lift each foot. If your horse demands you walk out and personally escort them from the furthest corner of their pasture, you might be getting a good hike in too.

Of course, there's a flip side to every wonderful trait about horses. That long walk to the back of the pasture tends to be a little less enjoyable when it's super hot, raining, or snowing. Likewise, when cleaning stalls in the frigid cold or high humidity, the pitchfork slipping out of your hands can be unbearable. There are flies, spiders, and all sorts of other bugs that you may have never needed to identify until now. Fans and heaters can be helpful, but there's still a lot of outdoor activity when working with horses.

There will be days when you won't want to drag yourself down to the barn to deal with it all. In fact, there will be days when you would rather be anywhere in the entire world than freezing or roasting in a stinky barn. Your back and arms will be sore. You won't be in the mood. You might have a thousand other things to do. But this large beast is depending on you to take care of him.

And yes, there's no denying that horses are not just time consuming but expensive also. Nearly every horse person has gone into the ownership process with the naive thought, "Maybe he'll be an easy keeper! Then I can just feed him a supplemental complete feed, and he can be on 24 hour turnout. All of that grass will keep him fat and happy."

I have had one horse that was an easy keeper. However, since he was out in the field all the time, we had to constantly keep the field mowed so that he wouldn't overindulge in grass and become ill. The fence line had to be checked daily, and any repairs had to be immediate. His water trough still had to be dumped, cleaned, and refilled. His shelter had to be mucked out daily because manure is an ideal breeding ground for flies and other pests.

He had specific health needs as an outdoor horse as well. I had to ensure he was dewormed regularly to prevent parasite build up. Running free and happy in the field caused him to wear down his shoes quickly (or leave them behind in a particularly sticky patch of mud), which meant a pricey farrier bill every six weeks. He was also what we called a "scratch and ding wizard" because he was always coming in from the field with some weird minor flesh wound that would require immediate care.

Therefore, this is your official warning to abandon the hope that your horse will be inexpensive. Feed, hay, bedding, supplements, maintenance of the field and enclosure, vets, farriers, trainers, and all of the supplies such as buckets, wheelbarrows, and pitchforks add up over time. Don't worry. We'll get into a detailed breakdown of costs and equipment in a later section. For now, just rest assured that the old adage is true: There really and truly is no such thing as a free horse.

Horses are also, sadly, very fragile. Their long limbs are easily injured. It's unlikely and even dangerous to ask them to lie down to recover, which means some physical injuries have no hope of healing. They have very sensitive stomachs and are unable to vomit which means a minor tummy ache can turn into life-threatening colic in the blink of an eye. With proper care, horses can live well into their 30s, but one simple accident can end not only their career, but their life.

It's impossible to compare the equine lifestyle to that of any other animal. Horses are amazing companions, providing physical activity opportunities and emotional support for their humans. At the same time, they require full dedication to keep them well. This involves a heavy investment of time and money, which can become very stressful over time. And even when you do absolutely everything right, there are still times when we need to accept that horses are oddly delicate for such large, powerful beasts.

My goal is not to frighten you or make horse ownership sound like a long, miserable disaster. Like any other journey we make in life, there are both wonderful and heart-breaking moments. Some horses live a long, beautiful life without incident, and other horses' lives are cut tragically short. Again, you may ask yourself, "Is it worth it?" I have obviously said, "Yes, it's worth It," several times, but only you can tell if you have the fortitude to take on the responsibility of one of these amazing animals.

SECTION 2: WHAT HORSES REQUIRE OF THEIR OWNERS

When speaking to first-time prospective horse owners about whether they'll be able to provide everything their horse will require, the answer I receive is almost always a version of, "Sure! How hard can it be? We have a shed, a fence, and lots of grass! Everything a horse needs!"

With all due respect to everyone's best intentions, these are actually some of the lower-tier things that a horse will enjoy. While it's true that some horses will be generally pleased with the bare minimum of care, that "bare minimum" may extend much further than you're aware if your horse turns out to have hidden medical issues or personal preferences. Additionally, each aspect of horse care has many considerations that rely on a world of variables. Once you have accepted responsibility for a horse, you'll need to provide the care they require, so it's best to be aware of all of the things that entails right off the bat.

Let's break it down piece by piece:

Water

In an average 24-hour period, a horse will consume between 6 and 10 gallons of water. This can increase dramatically in hot weather or after hard work.

So how are you going to supply this water?

When the horse is relaxing in their stall, a 10 gallon water bucket hung from the wall should be sufficient. You can buy these buckets for a relatively reasonable price at a farm supply store. But, like everything else, there are several things you need to keep in mind.

First, your horse will do everything possible to make his water as disgusting as possible. Nearly every horse person has experienced a horse filling his freshly-cleaned water bucket with manure, often right after it's been topped off. Horses will also stuff their hay and dribble grain in their water buckets, which when left overnight, makes a very strange and stinky brew. If your horse is a "recycler" (i.e.- he eats his own manure), you'll likely have to dump the contents and refill the bucket several times a day. Mares in heat may urinate in their water buckets as well.

Then, you have to consider the critter population of your barn. Despite anyone's best attempts, horse owners are apt to find all sorts of specimens floating in water buckets and troughs. I personally have removed squirrels, baby opossum, mice, toads, moths, wasps, spiders, and even a large and still very much alive cockroach. It is always deeply unpleasant to dispose of these contents, plus, you will need to thoroughly sanitize the bucket before you allow your horse to drink out of it again due to the risks of contamination.

Ofcourse, there's the business of the horse itself. Some horses find water buckets an irresistible play thing. They'll bat them around with their heads, kick at them with their hooves, and rub all of their itchy places against them. You may find your buckets in strange places, or split, spilt, and shattered after no time at all.

If your barnyard has been plumbed with running water pipes and electricity, automatic waterers are a very handy invention. With automatic waterers, you'll never have to worry about your horse running out of water... unless the power goes off for a significant amount of time, or your horse manages to fill it with so much debris that the unit shorts.

These units aren't as portable and easy to dump, clean, and refill as traditional buckets, and they still get their fair share of manure and critter accidents. However, your horse will have constant access to fresh water, and they won't have the option of tossing it out of their stall or stomping it into a million pieces.

For horses that spend a significant amount of time outside, troughs are a popular choice. It would be lovely if horse owners could buy a giant trough, fill it to the brim with water, and not worry about it for a few days. But again, things fall in. From manure to wildlife, a trough needs to be checked several times a day to ensure it's clean.

Furthermore, troughs need to be dumped and cleaned frequently. Much like a pond, or even an aquarium, things start to grow in a trough over time. Regardless of how meticulous you are, it's impossible to escape biology, and you'll find algae and slime coating the inside of your trough after a day or two. For this reason, I recommend buying a trough that you are physically capable of tipping and dumping so you can keep it clean at all times.

Some horses don't mind drinking dirty water. Others will absolutely refuse to touch water if there's a single strand of hay floating in it. Though a horse can survive for days and weeks without food, they can start showing signs of distress after just a day without water. Horses depend on water to keep their digestive systems moving to help flush down the massive amounts of forage they need to stay alive (don't worry- we'll get to the food part shortly). Depriving a horse of water can lead to impaction colic, in which their intestines become blocked, as well as musculoskeletal issues, such as sporadic tying up, a condition in which the large muscles of a horse's hindquarters seem to lock and become painful. Therefore, it is extremely important that a horse has a constant supply of fresh water.

And those of you who live in areas that experience freezing winters will enjoy an extra challenge: ice. Ice will form on water buckets and troughs very quickly. Heated buckets and waterproof heaters that can be dropped into buckets or troughs are available, but these require an electrical source. Some barn owners use a permanently mounted rubber thermal sleeve to prevent ice buildup, and then manually break the ice each morning with a hammer or mallet. I personally find that a well-placed kick on the side of the bucket tends to break up the ice nicely, as well as provides a fun cardio kickboxing type workout, but most people prefer hand tools.

Roughage

Entire volumes have been written about how to feed horses, and truthfully, there is a lot to learn and consider on the topic.

Horses require at least 1% of their body weight in quality roughage each day. When it's cold outside, that number jumps to a minimum of 2%. Working horses will also need more roughage. That means a 1000 pound horse will require 10 pounds of grass and/or hay each day. Bear in mind that a typical bale of hay weighs between 50 and 75 pounds; therefore, a horse can easily munch their way through a bale of hay in a day or two. Use this value to calculate a month's or year's worth of hay to get the full picture of how many hay bales you'll need to keep on hand at all times.

Roughage is non-negotiable for horses. They need it to keep their digestive tract moving. That being said, there are many ways to get the recommended quantity.

First, and least expensive, is pasture. Grass and leafy green things are full of the nutrients horses need to thrive. Your pasture provides the natural diet of horses, and they'll be content to chomp on a field all day. Seems easy enough, right?

Unfortunately, there are quite a few things you'll need to consider before you throw your horse outside all day and wish him happy eating. There are many plants that are toxic to horses and can make them extremely ill or be fatal if eaten. You'll need to take the time to identify which of your area's native plants can be harmful and remove them before your horse is turned out.

There's also too much of a good thing when it comes to horses and food. Horses who eat too much lush grass are at risk for colic. Unlike cows and other ruminants, horses only have one stomach. Ruminants have the ability to regurgitate their cud for additional chewing and digestion, but horses can't regurgitate or vomit at all. As a result, an upset stomach can lead to a full-blown colic episode very quickly.

Laminitis is also a risk for horses who indulge in too much food. The lamina is the soft tissue layer that helps connect the bone of the leg to the hoof. Horses who eat more than their bodies can handle will experience sudden swelling of the laminae. Not only is this incredibly painful, but allowing the condition to continue without treatment can permanently damage the structure of the horse's hoof and lower leg.

Additionally, horses who become overweight are more prone to insulin resistance. Essentially, this is like Type 2 diabetes in a horse. Insulin resistance can also lead to laminitis, as well as excessive drinking, urination, and fat deposits along the neck and hindquarters.

In fact, many experts refuse to allow their horses to graze during afternoons when the sugar content in pastures is at its highest. Instead, they'll turn their horses out overnight, or in the early morning, or evening hours, to ensure they're getting the nutrition they need without worrying about potential overdosing on natural sugars.

The next option for providing roughage is hay. But beware: not all hay is created equally. It's important that you choose hay that has been specifically cut and stored for horses, as this hay will be free of any molds, moisture, or dust that can be toxic to horses. Additionally, there are actually different types of hay. Alfalfa and clover are actually legume hay, while timothy, bluegrass, and orchard are all grass hay. Each type of hay has a different nutritional profile based on the various levels of moisture, crude protein, calcium, and mineral content.

Legume hay is higher in protein and calcium, which means it's richer and denser. Like too much access to pasture, this can cause problems. Some owners have identified that legume hay makes their horses "hotter", meaning they have excess energy. Unless your horse has a hard time maintaining body condition or has a heavy workload, a lot of legume hay can have a similar effect to a large candy bar on a small child.

Grass hay, on the other hand, is higher in fiber but contains lower levels of other nutrients. This means horses have to eat more grass-based hay to get the nutrients they need, but that can be an advantage to horses who spend most of their day inside. The fiber encourages motility in their digestive tracts, which helps mitigate colic and maintain ideal health.

Hay grows in cycles referred to as "cuttings". First cutting produces the early spring hay which tends to be coarse. As the growing season continues, the cuttings tend to be more fine and dense. You may find that you need to feed more of the stemmy, stalky first cutting than the silky, nutritious second cutting and beyond. Older horses with fewer teeth may have difficulty with first cutting hay but will happily munch on second or third cutting hay from the same field.

Generally speaking, hay is easy to come by, but occasionally, environmental factors such as drought or flooding will create a hay blight. You may also find that your horse has a difficult time eating hay, perhaps due to problems with their mouth or teeth, or due to being a choke risk. Just like humans, horses can get food stuck in their esophagus. Unlike in humans, we can't simply perform the Heimlich maneuver on a horse to help them out. They've got several feet of esophagus to coax a blockage through, and then there's the problematic mechanics of that solution.

These are just a few of the reasons that owners might choose to explore different types of roughage. Beet pulp and alfalfa cubes are two examples of commercially available roughage for horses. Beet pulp is often used to supplement fiber intake for horses with a variety of medical conditions that would preclude them from eating hay, including breathing issues, lack of teeth, and metabolic conditions. Alfalfa cubes are used in similar situations for horses who need a denser nutritional content in their roughage supplements. Both beet pulp and alfalfa cubes should be soaked thoroughly before being fed to horses to help them chew and swallow the coarse material.

Grain

A quick trip to the feed mill or farm supply shop will show you that there are seemingly endless options when it comes to a pellet feed for your horse. Choosing the right one may seem like a daunting task.

My personal recommendation is to find out what your horse is eating right now and continue that program, unless you or your vet see any reason to make changes. There are many things that are going to be changing in a horse's life when he leaves his current home to live with you. For example, the pasture and hay will be different. Every experiment requires a control, so my suggestion is to not change grain right away unless there is a very strong reason to do so.

The three main considerations of pellet horse feed are protein, fat, and fiber. There is some debate as to whether horses require more protein or fat, and truthfully, it really depends on the horse and their job. A horse who spends his days leisurely strolling through the pasture will need far less protein and fiber since he's already getting it from the grass. A hard keeping Thoroughbred who loses his marbles and insists on coming inside every time the bugs get aggressive will need far more protein and fiber. He'll likely need more fat too, especially if he's doing a lot of work throughout the day.

Horse feed manufacturers have helpfully labeled their formulas with the type of situation their feed is intended to support. For example, you'll see "Senior Feed", "Mare and Foal Feed", and "High Performance Feed". Always read the tags. Different brands have different formulas, and the levels of nutrition in one brand's "Senior" blend, for example, might be very different from another brand.

One very important thing to note is that the percentages and benefits touted by each type of horse feed are based on the serving directions printed on the bag. If you feed your horse less than the serving directions, you may not see the miraculous advantages claimed by each brand.

When in doubt, talk to your vet. Your vet will be able to look at your horse and evaluate their overall body condition. They'll also be able to take blood samples to find possible nutrient deficiencies.

If you decide to make changes to your horse's feed, remember to go slow. This is true for everything your horse eats including pasture, hay, and hay substitutes. That incredibly sensitive digestive tract that keeps popping up is once again an important reason to slowly make changes to your horse's feed routine. The general guideline is to replace ¼ of a ration per day with the new item, but always check with your vet for specific recommendations.

Medical Care

A solid relationship with a good, thorough veterinarian is essential. Horses are masters of appearing with mysterious maladies. From cuts and scrapes, to lameness and beyond, horses manage to get into all sorts of trouble.

It is a fantastic idea to start hunting for a vet before you even purchase a horse. There may be a variety of vets who service your area, but contacting them before your horse comes home allows you to ensure they are taking new patients and learn more about their practice. Do they have digital imaging equipment? Do they offer dental services? Can they provide chiropractic services? Are they more focused on lameness or reproductive services? How many vets are at the practice? What are their emergency policies and procedures? There is nothing as terrifying as having a horse in critical condition and attempting to frantically connect with a vet in your area.

In addition to tending to your horse in times of crisis, your vet will also be able to provide or recommend deworming programs, vaccination schedules, and long-term care regimens based on your horse's wellness needs. Deworming and vaccinations are very important for a horse's health. Horses can pick up all sorts of parasites when grazing in even the most meticulously kept field, and vaccinations protect against highly communicable diseases that can be spread by common insects and directly between horses. Your vet can advise you as to which dewormers and vaccinations are essential in your area.

In fact, some horse owners prefer to have their vet look at their horse before they even make the first payment. In what is called a "Pre-Purchase Exam," or PPE, the vet will evaluate your prospective horse's conformation, hooves, teeth, conduct a full lameness exam, and may even take x-rays to bring to light any issues that might be lurking in the background. The purpose of a PPE is not to expose the dishonesty of the previous owner, as they may not even know about a horse's issues. Instead, a PPE will prepare you for the level of care a horse will need once it comes home. You will then be able to make a decision as to whether this horse and its needs will fit into your lifestyle and abilities or not.

Once a vet has made their recommendations, a lot of daily medical care for horses can be accomplished at home. You may find yourself cold hosing swollen legs, applying salve and fresh bandages to wounds, or soaking and packing Epsom salts into a lingering hoof abscess. This is all part of the territory when you own a horse. You'll learn how to administer paste medications orally or crush up pills in their feed. You may even learn how to give intramuscular and subcutaneous injections to provide your horse with the treatment they need to stay well.

If you are not comfortable with needles, blood, and assorted bodily fluids, that doesn't mean you can't have a horse. In these instances, you'll want to find someone who can provide 24 hour, 7 day a week support for your horse. A boarding facility that is willing to provide medical care is one option for finding assistance.

Farrier Services

There's a common saying in the horse community: "No hoof, no horse." Truer words have never been spoken.

Foot injuries to a horse are not only painful, but if not attended to can be career ending or even life-threatening. While you can lie down on your sofa with your foot propped up until you heal, horses don't have that luxury. They can lie down, but not for long periods of time. Furthermore, the process of getting up from a prone position requires a lot of effort for horses. You can't just ask a horse to stay off its foot for four weeks.

Therefore, good hoof care is absolutely essential. Hooves are made of a fingernail-like material, and they grow just like fingernails do. When they get too long, they need to be trimmed.

Some people argue that wild horses don't need farriers, so why should their domesticated horses? Wild horses often travel up to 20 miles a day on rugged terrain to find enough food and water, which naturally wears down their hooves. Chances are your horse is not wearing down his feet at the same rate as a wild horse.

Just like humans, all horses move a little differently. If you and a friend bought the same pair of sneakers and wore them for a year, the tread patterns would look different from each other. Your farrier can evaluate your horse's movement and trim their hooves to allow them to move more freely. In fact, a lot of lameness issues can be corrected or relieved with appropriate trimming and horse shoes.

A good farrier won't just trim a hoof; they'll take a look at your horse's conformation, body type, work load, and wear patterns on their hooves or shoes to ensure their work fully supports the horse going forward. They'll evaluate angles and shapes and use a variety of tools to take accurate measurements. I once had a farrier who was able to diagnose my back pain from the wear patterns on my horse's shoes and was able to rebalance both my horse and myself with corrective shoeing. In order to keep your horses healthy, happy, and moving well, a good farrier is non-negotiable.

Attention

For those who find themselves more or less obsessed with horses, this one may seem strange. Who *wouldn't* give their horse endless attention? My experiences have shown me that there are a lot of people who believe horses are field decorations, lawn ornaments, or very pretty lawnmowers. It's not that they dislike their horses, they just don't feel that they require much attention.

When I say "attention", I don't necessarily mean you need to snuggle with your horse all the time. Horses are very social animals. As herd animals, they require some form of interaction. It's not uncommon to find a bonded pair of horses, even in the wild. They create intricate social structures within their herds, and they require some form of interaction in order to be happy. In the absence of an equine companion, horses can bond with other animals such as goats or dogs.

Your experience with your horse will be much more enjoyable if you take the time to form a bond with your horse. There are seemingly infinite "horsemanship gurus" out there who provide tips and tricks for creating the ideal relationship with your horse, but it all boils down to one common action: paying attention to your horse.

The more time you spend with your horse, the more you'll learn about them. Domestic horses tend to be creatures of habit and will develop their own routines. The more you observe and understand their routines, the more likely you will be able to identify when anything is off with your companion. Changes in eating, drinking, manure production, or energy levels can be signs of a medical issue, so catching these strange variances early could save your horse's life.

Take the time to groom them daily. Grooming helps keep the horse's skin and coat healthy and gives you the opportunity to check them over for bumps and cuts or any other unusual skin disturbances. Horses are prone to all sorts of skin issues, such as rain rot, ringworm, and scratches, a type of dermatitis affecting the skin around the lower leg and hoof. These bacterial and fungal infections can cause your horse significant discomfort and can require extensive treatment. The good news is that regular grooming can help you identify these issues at the onset before they become too difficult to manage with over the counter solutions.

Regularly spending time with your horse will also improve your ability to handle them. The easiest way to gain your horse's trust is by spending time with them. Once your horse appreciates who you are and that you have their best interest in mind, it will be much easier to lead them around, hold them for the vet and farrier, and train them to do whatever you wish to accomplish together.

Author's Anecdote: Absolutely Look a Gift Horse in the Mouth... and Everywhere Else

When I was given my Thoroughbred gelding, Red, I knew I had a lot of work to do, but it wasn't until I brought him home that I discovered how much needed to be done. He had been living in a field for four months. He'd had access to grass and water, but that was about it.

Not only did he need to gain about 400-500 pounds to be healthy, but he was essentially hairless due to the massive coating of rain rot scabs across his back, hindquarters, and barrel. His legs were oozing from scratches sores that had become infected. His teeth and hooves were overgrown, which meant he had trouble eating the food we provided him, and he walked with careful, mincing steps.

I was very careful about introducing grain to him to avoid upsetting his tummy. He got a full round of vaccinations and dewormers. The vet ran blood tests to see what issues he might have and took care of his teeth with a process known as "floating" in which teeth are filed down to create adequate chewing area and take care of any sharp bits that are poking the mouth or tongue. I spent months using medication and special shampoos on his coat to help kill the fungus and regrow healthy skin and hair. He was treated for ulcers, and I gave him supplements designed to help him recover.

All told, bringing Red back to full health required thousands of dollars, several vet visits, and months of careful farrier work. The first few months, I would work a full day at my regular job then drive an hour to the barn where Red was boarded, do my barn chores and spend several hours working with him to clean his skin and build a good relationship with him. It was not easy, and there were several times when I broke down in tears on my long drive home because I wasn't sure how things were going to turn out.

The people who had him before me were not mean people. They had three small ponies who were fat and sassy just as they stood. They simply weren't aware that different horses have different needs. When I pointed out some of the issues Red was experiencing, they were absolutely appalled and ashamed of themselves. They simply didn't know.

Something as simple as spending fifteen minutes a day with your horse can make you more aware of how they're feeling. As you spend time with your horse, you'll notice when they're gaining or losing weight so you can adjust their diet accordingly. When you groom them, you'll feel any changes in the texture or thickness of their coat. Picking their hooves will allow you to assess any cracks, bruises, or abscesses that may need attention.

Today, Red is a thriving middle aged horse. He still requires a lot of work to keep him in good shape. Due to his previous starvation, it's incredibly hard to keep weight on him. But he's an amazing companion-- a sweet, level-headed horse who enjoys cuddles and treats equally. He's spent some time doing equine therapy work with disadvantaged children, and he's even done some modeling!

In short, just a little care can go a long way in keeping your horse healthy and happy. That's not to say you have to eat and sleep in your horse's stall or pasture, but you will need to attend to your horse more frequently than you might expect.

If any of these caretaking practices are not ideal for your lifestyle, there are options. The first, of course, is to pass on adding a horse to your list of commitments, but there are situations in which that is impossible. Full board, partial leases, and hiring a caretaker are all ways your horse can get additional attention while you balance the other details of your life. Just remember-- you have a choice in adding a horse to your life, but the horse does not.

Now that you know what a horse needs to stay alive and well, we'll take a look at how to select and create the perfect environment for your horse. Your horse's home is the common factor between all of these caretaking needs and responsibilities, so it's important that your horse's home helps you provide them with all of the things needed to keep them safe and sound for a long time to come.

SECTION 3: CHOOSING THE RIGHT HOME FOR YOUR HORSE

So far, we've mentioned what your horse needs, but we haven't specified where you're going to put everything.

Depending on where you live, this decision may be made for you. If you live in a large metropolitan area, for example, there's no way you can simply make room for a horse in your backyard-- if you even have a backyard. And in suburban areas, zoning regulations and Homeowner Association (HOA) guidelines are likely going to squelch any notion you had of building a stall for your horse in your garage.

However, for those who live outside city limits, the options open up. There are still a few factors that may prevent you from having a horse at home, such as limited land or the expense associated with creating the perfect living arrangements for your horse.

In this section, we'll take a look at exactly what a horse needs when it comes to their living situation. From stalls to fences and everything in between, there are certain things your horse will need in order to be completely comfortable.

As I have mentioned several times throughout this book, always bear in mind that different horses will have different needs. It may seem as though I'm being super repetitive on this point, but even as a seasoned equestrian, it's sometimes hard for me to remember that not all horses are willing to spend half a day outside roaming freely, or that some horses become very anxious if they're kept inside for too long. There comes a point when we've all thrown our hands in the air in exasperation, ditched all of our best intentions, and made do with whatever preferences the horse has.

Therefore, it's important to create a master plan for your horse's habitat with the idea in the back of your mind that you may need to come up with options. We'll look at two scenarios: keeping your horse at home versus boarding him. There are plenty of things to think about in each case, but don't worry- we'll look at the pros and cons of each, as well as create a list of questions to ask yourself and whomever you choose to board with.

Chapter 1: The Ideal Horse Habitat

You've probably heard your horsey friends or trainer joke that the best way to keep a horse would be in a bubble. This is because horses seem to find every possible way to injure themselves when kept in a stall. From finding sharp edges that are unseen to the human eye to getting cast, which is when a horse lies down and can't get up due to how they're wedged against a wall. Horses are very creative at damaging themselves.

Of course, they can find interesting ways to injure themselves in the field as well. Pulled tendons, bruised hooves, and weird scrapes and lacerations are just some of the "fun" things you can find on your horse when you bring them in from the field.

Therefore, the first thing you should ask yourself about any space in which you plan to keep your horse is, "Is it safe?" You don't need a shiny, fancy barn full of giant box stalls, as long as the environment in which you keep your horse is safe. That means fences, stalls, shelters, and even the land itself need to be in good repair. You'll need to check for holes, broken boards and posts, sharp edges, nails or screws that might be poking out, downed branches, leaks, cracks, and so forth. Even a daily microscopic inspection might not prevent some of the mischief horses can get into, but filling in holes in the pasture and testing the fence line is one place to start to mitigate an expensive tragedy.

So how much room do you need for a horse? The general rule is an acre of land per horse, but that only takes into consideration the amount of space a horse needs for grazing. Two acres for the first horse and one acre for every subsequent horse is even better, as this allows the horses room to roam as a herd and cuts back on the risk of overgrazing.

You may look at your field and think, "There's no way a horse could graze that bald," but you might be surprised at what a diligent horse can do to a pasture. Running and rolling will churn up dirt, and when it's wet that means turning a lush pasture into a useless mudpit. If it's very rainy or very dry, your overgrown field can quickly turn into a dirt lot under the hooves and teeth of a horse.

Additionally, there are plants that horses simply will not eat. You'll need to mow or bush hog those from time to time to get them under control. It can be very easy to "lose" a small pony in a thicket of tall weeds. Don't worry-- they'll reappear in time for their next meal, but you'll want to check them over for ticks or other problematic bugs that lurk in the overgrown areas.

From the pasture, we move on to the shelter aspect. Even horses who are content to live outside all day and night will need some form of shelter to protect themselves from the heat, sun, wind, rain, and snow. Depending on your location, you may not experience all of these weather conditions, but horses will enjoy a respite from standing in the open air all day. Whether to get away from insects, or to feel safe while enjoying a nice nap, your horse will be grateful for shelter.

Shelter doesn't always have to mean a stall. Some horses are quite content with a simple three-walled run-in with a roof that protects them from the elements. Others enjoy the security of a stall. The ideal situation is both: a pasture where they can stretch their legs, snack on grass, and socialize, complimented by a large, airy stall in which they can snooze and feel safe.

The size of the stall is also important. An average sized horse of around 1,000 pounds will need a stall that is at least 12 feet by 12 feet. This gives them plenty of room to turn around, lie down, stand back up, and move enough to keep them comfortable. Small horses can get by with smaller stalls, especially if they have plenty of exercise throughout the day.

The main challenge of keeping horses in stalls is boredom. Horses are designed to roam, forage for roughage, and socialize. Unfortunately, it's not always practical to recreate a wild horse's kingdom in our own backyards, regardless of how much land you may have. Most domesticated horses enjoy a balance of turnout in a pasture and time in the stall. This helps landowners rotate pastures between multiple horses or other animals. Plus, it's admittedly very convenient to have your horse in a stall when the vet or farrier is visiting. If you plan on riding or exercising your horse, it's also nice to have a stall or other enclosed space where you can groom them, get them tacked up, and prepare for the work ahead of you.

Again, a stall doesn't have to be a fancy highly-varnished affair. I've seen stalls made out of cattle panels, some constructed from reconfigurable fiberglass and steel bar panels, and homemade stalls from strong posts and 2x6 panelling.

No matter what type of construction you use, airflow in your barn and stalls is extremely important. Horse urine is high in ammonia, and manure doesn't exactly smell wonderful. When it's hot or cold, the air circulation in your horse's enclosure is not only going to keep the stink down, but help you manage the temperature as well. Therefore, if you decide to build a barn or multi-horse enclosure, consider windows or Dutch doors as a way to encourage greater airflow. If you have multiple stalls, consider extending the walls between them high enough to dissuade horses from visiting their neighbors, rather than building them all the way to the ceiling. Many stalls are constructed with bars or mesh across the front to not only allow horses to see out and humans to see in, but to increase air circulation throughout the entire space.

As mentioned, the urine and manure smells will become overwhelming very quickly, so have a plan in place for regular removal and disposal of your horse's waste. Some locations have specific requirements as to where manure can be disposed of in relation to human dwellings, roadways, or water sources, so be aware of those regulations before you start dumping. You may also want to encourage your local gardening friends to tap into your endless source of high-quality organic fertilizer!

Then comes the matter of fencing. The only type of fencing most horse experts would strictly advise against is barbed wire. There are many types of fencing available today, including electrified webbing, high tensile wire, wooden post-and-board, vinyl strips or planks, and more. Some horse owners set up temporary grazing areas with electrified braided rope and QuikFence spikes, even at home, because they're easily moved to prevent overgrazing.

Most horses will respect the visual cue of a fence line, though some require at least one electrified line to remind them to stay within the lines. Also, an electric fence doesn't have to be turned up to extreme levels to coax most horses into obedience. Some barns have solar-powered, portable electric units that are used only when certain horses are turned out or to keep predators out of the field at night. All of this is to say that your fencing doesn't have to be extremely elaborate, as long as it's functional and safe.

The main thing to consider regarding fence safety is how the fencing material will respond if a 1,000 pound beast moving at 25 miles per hour (or faster) crashes into it. There's no way to avoid damage to the fence or your horse, but the type of fencing you have can help prevent tragedy. This is why barbed wire is highly advised against since a horse's body slamming into this type of fencing can result in the horse becoming tangled, leading to multiple lacerations as a possible consequence.

Horses also like to put their heads and hooves through fences. Materials like vinyl and webbing tend to be more forgiving to horses who have this type of tendency. Horses have been known to dangle from a horse shoe or hog-tie themselves in high tensile wire fences. While this is certainly scary for everyone involved and not to be taken lightly, the benefit of this fencing type is that it can be easily cut with heavy duty wire cutters to release the horse and be repaired once the horse is safe and sound. I personally have only had to do this twice in the past 30 years, though my mentor speaks fondly of a horse she had who would get the fence tangled in his shoes at least once a month but had the good sense to stand patiently until someone could pull on the wire to free him.

Therefore, make sure your fencing is safe and that your horse respects it, and choose something that is easily repaired because you may need to repair it more frequently than you might anticipate.

The last element of your horse's ideal habitat is a water source . We've already discussed the importance of your horse having access to water, but let's step back and consider how you're going to get the water to him. Nearly every barn I've worked at, even the small backyard facilities with just two stalls, have a water source inside the barn. This means getting the area plumbed with a spigot or well pump, so you can easily refill buckets or troughs without running back and forth from the house for gallon after gallon of water.

Some smaller facilities have run a very long hose from the house to the barnyard which is also acceptable. The only issue with this plan is making sure the hose doesn't freeze when the temperature drops. If you go with this plan, you might choose to bring the hose inside when it's not in use, or meticulously drain the hose after each use. Heated hoses are another option, though they tend to be a bit pricey.

Natural water sources, such as ponds or creeks, aren't very popular in my area, but I am acquainted with many horse owners in other states who enjoy such amenities. If you are lucky enough to have a reliable natural water source, just be sure to test the water frequently to make sure it's drinkable and inspect the source often. Something as simple and unavoidable as a deer carcass upstream can pollute your horses' water and make them very sick, which means you'll need to be aware and come up with an alternate solution right away.

So there you have it. The basic, ideal horse habitat includes at least an acre to graze and play on, shelter, fencing, and a source of water. It sounds so simple when boiled down to just those elements, yet anyone who has had a horse run through a fence line or get cast in his stall will tell you that these are more than enough features to keep up with at once.

The good news is that you don't necessarily have to do this alone. In some areas, boarding a horse at a professionally maintained facility is a great compromise for those who don't have the time, energy, carpentry know-how, or money to keep their horses at home. Of course, you'll still want to look for these main factors and gauge how appropriate each is for your horse. Let's continue our inspection of horse habitats by looking at the pros and cons of boarding versus keeping your horse at home.

Chapter 2: Should I Keep My Horse at Home or Board It?

Over the past several chapters, we've looked at what a horse needs to be content and in good condition. Now it's time to take a look at the human component of the equine relationship. Armed with these details regarding horse care, how do you feel? Are you as confident and eager as ever to add a horse to your family? Or are you starting to feel a bit of doubt and worry creeping in? Maybe you feel completely intimidated by what you've read so far.

All of these are perfectly natural, and you may experience each emotion in varying waves. After 30 years with horses, I still feel anxious and overwhelmed from time to time, especially when things aren't going according to routine.

The good news is that you don't have to take this on alone. In fact, as mentioned earlier, you may not have the option to do so. Boarding your horse at a facility other than your home can be an amazing opportunity, even if you do have the ability to keep a horse in your own backyard.

Having worked at dozens of facilities, including boarding barns with 100 stalls or more, and small backyard barns housing just a horse or two, I can confirm that there are advantages and disadvantages to both options. Let's take a look at some of the main things to consider when choosing the perfect home for your horse. And for those of you who have no choice but to board, this section will give you some insight into what to look for in a prospective boarding facility.

Advantages of Keeping Your Horse at Home

If you are the type of person who enjoys having control over every aspect of your life, keeping your horse at home may be ideal. When you keep your horse at home, you have around-the-clock access to your horse. If you want to ride at midnight, you can. It's your horse, your property, and your time. You can clean your stalls any time of day and turn your horses out whenever you want. You can set whatever schedule works for you and your horses.

In most cases, you will be the only person to take care of your horse unless you specifically authorize someone else to help you out such as a family member or trusted friend. This means you'll have complete control over the care your horse receives. You can choose how much bedding you put in your horse's stall. You can select what type of hay you purchase, what time of day they get fed, and when they get supplements. You get to put them on the deworming and vaccination schedule of your choice.

Also, you can choose your own farrier, vet, and schedule them whenever your schedules allow. You can select the trainer you want to work with and decide whether you're going to take your horse to their facility for lessons, or whether you want them to come to you. Some trainers will travel, though they may charge an additional fee. The important thing to keep in mind is that you have complete freedom to choose the care team to support you and your horse.

For many equestrians, another advantage to keeping your horse at home is the peace and quiet of solitude. You don't have to share the barn with anyone else. No one will be hanging around, watching you ride, borrowing your equipment, or using the hose when you need to use the hose. If something gets lost, you know exactly who to blame. If you don't feel like talking to anyone, no worries because there's no one around to talk to anyway.

Disadvantages of Keeping Your Horse at Home

If all of that sounds pretty good to you, then you might just be a true dyed-in-the-wool horse person. But hold on, there are a few flip sides to all of those major advantages.

First of all, having complete solo care of your horse means that everything is your responsibility. For example, you'll need to find a hay supplier. You'll need to find a way to get the hay from their field to your barn. You'll need to stack the hay. You'll need to pull bales of hay when it's time to feed them and check them for mold and dust.

You'll need to make all of the decisions in your barn. What type of bedding will you use? Where will you keep it? Where are you going to keep your equipment? How are you going to store your feed? What will your feeding schedule look like? How many hours will you turn your horse out? At what time of day? Where are you going to ride or work with your horse?

The responsibility extends past the mere duties and decisions, and into the expenses. How are you going to pay for everything? Budgeting for things like a $100 farrier bill each month, a $20 bag of feed each week, and a $6 bale of hay every day is pretty straightforward, but how are you going to budget for unexpected situations? Even the most deliberate budgeting can be thrown for a loop with a $3000 vet bill or $1000 in fence repairs when a storm blows a tree down in your pastures.

You will be responsible for all maintenance too. If you're comfortable with basic tools such as hammers, nails, screws and screwdrivers, hand saws, and wire cutters, you're prepared to handle most of the basics. There's an old saying that "horse people can solve just about any problem with duct tape and baling twine", and to a point, that's very true. Both are strong products that tend to be abundant in a barn setting. When combined with a little creativity and tenacity, they can create a temporary fix for many situations. Check out the Resources section for links giving some insight on this topic, if you're curious!

But real repairs require real supplies,skill, andmoney. You'll need to learn how to repair fence posts and fence lines, stalls, stall doors, gates, gate latches, hoses, water pumps, and more. You'll need to understand how to "horse proof" your property from bush hogging the pastures when they start to grow too high to finding sharp edges in your barn and wrapping duct tape around them. Even things that you think would already be horse-proof can be dangerous. For example, the handle loops on their water buckets can easily jab an eye or scratch their face, so many barn owners wrap duct tape around these loops to prevent injury. As the steward for your horse, it is your responsibility to find these problems, correct them, and deal with the consequences all at once.

You'll also need to find reliable resources for the supplies you need for your horse. That means a regular source of feed, hay, bedding, and footing, if you choose to set up an arena on your property for riding. Bear in mind that feed stores or farm supply shops will run out of your particular brand from time to time. There is a time in each horse owner's life when they stand in silent disbelief at the feed store, dumbstruck by the sight of empty racks where what you need should be. How can they possibly run out of all the bedding, feed, or supplement you need? You'll feel yourself break into a cold sweat as you try to consider work arounds, or other nearby supply resources. Are you the type to think fast in situations like this, or will you succumb to anxiety?

Many people avoid this anxiety by buying their supplies in bulk. They buy footing and bedding by the dump truck load and multiple bags of feed at a time. They'll purchase hundreds of bales of hay at once. This is a fantastic idea, as it gives you time to plan ahead for the next time you'll need to stock up. At the same time, it's important to note that all of these things need to be stored in a dry place out of direct sunlight. Do you have room to stack 100 bales of hay? Do you have a large enough airtight, waterproof container to store multiple bags of feed? Buying supplies for your horse in large quantities makes a lot of sense and relieves stress, but you'll need a sufficient amount of room and a plan to keep everything stored appropriately.

Another thing you'll need to plan for is manure management. A 1,000 pound horse will produce over 50 pounds of manure each day. Where are you going to put this waste once it's removed from the stall or the pasture? Occasionally, you can pawn it off on others. Frequently, barns have standing agreements with local farmers that they may help themselves to the manure pile whenever they like. Some horse owners will post "Free Manure" ads on community selling walls and bulletin boards when the pile starts to get out of control. Another option is to buy a spreader attachment for your tractor so you can churn it and cure it in a pasture that is currently out of rotation. That means that your manure would be spread in the field your horses aren't currently using.

In addition to all of these logistics, you'll need to consider your lifestyle. Does your schedule allow you to be at home every day at roughly the same time to keep your horse on a familiar routine? Do you have someone who can help you out if you become ill or injured? Do you enjoy traveling and going on vacations? If having your time available as you wish is important to you, it may not be a good idea to keep a horse at home. However, if your partner or the individuals who share your home are pretty reliable, you can achieve some flexibility. Some families have wonderful bonding experiences when taking care of the horses together. On the other hand, if you already feel stressed from running kids to school and practice, getting to work, getting meals on the table, attending appointments, and more, you might find that adding a horse to the mix only makes things feel more hectic.

Lastly, you'll need to change your insurance policy to account for your horse. What this entails varies greatly from location to location, so if you plan to add a horse to the property on which you reside, be sure to speak to your home insurance agent about next steps. You'll need insurance not just for the property and structures, but for your belongings. Your locality may also require liability insurance for scenarios such as your horse getting loose. You may also need to be insured against any accidents that happen on your property as a result of a guest interacting with your horse, such as a friend getting bitten when feeding your horse a treat. Some states require legal notification signs to be hung in a very visible place, while others require "Errors and Omissions" coverage. Find out what you need to know about insurance before you bring your equine friend home.

Advantages of Boarding Your Horse

As you can gather, having a horse at home will demand a lot from you starting with your time, energy, and money. For this reason, many horse owners -- even those who do have the land and the means to keep a horse at home -- prefer to board their horses at a facility.

The premise for boarding is simple. Find a facility that has available room, and pay a certain amount each month for what is essentially your horse's room and board. There are different types of board, however, so be sure to investigate thoroughly before signing a contract.

"Full board" refers to a boarding arrangement in which the daily basic needs are taken care of: your horse will be fed the same hay and grain that every other horse in the barn eats at the same time each day by people employed by the barn. Your horse's stall will be cleaned regularly by a barn employee and bedding will be included in your boarding costs as well.

"Partial board" means that some things are taken care of, but you'll still be responsible for some of your horse's care. This varies from facility to facility. At one of the barns where I've kept my horses, for example, the partial board included twice daily feeding, hay, and bedding, but each horse's owner had to clean their horse's stalls and provide their own grain. If a barn advertises partial board, be sure to ask them what is and is not included.

"Self-care board" essentially means you're paying for the privilege of keeping your horse at that facility. You'll be responsible for feeding your horse, making sure they have water, sourcing your own hay, and cleaning their stall. You may also be asked to provide your own bedding. In some cases, owners at self-care facilities are asked to turn their horses out and bring them in themselves as well. When you see a barn advertising self-care boarding, assume that you will be responsible for everything involved in the daily care of your horse.

"Pasture board" means that your horse will live outside 24/7 usually with a herd of other horses. Pasture board can be ideal for some horses, but you'll want to discuss the specifics with the barn owner. Do the horses come in for grain? Are they outside in all types of weather? What if they need to be on stall rest due to a medical situation-- will there be room for them to come inside? How are farrier and vet appointments handled-- will someone at the facility bring your horse in for you? Is there a holding stall or area where you can tie your horse while waiting for your appointment? There are many strategic points that need to be considered with pasture board, but many horses enjoy the ability to roam as they please in their downtime.

As you can see, there are several different types of boarding. Some larger facilities may have all four types of contracts available. Full board is generally the most expensive option, while self-care and pasture board are at the least expensive end of the price range.

But all of these boarding options have a few things in common. Namely, you're not responsible for the facility. You may be responsible for the cost of repairs if your horse kicks through a wall, chews a fence board, or pulls the cross ties out of the wall, to name a few possible scenarios, but the daily ins and outs of keeping the property running properly are not your responsibility. You are not required to make sure the arena has enough footing. You will not need to fix the water pump. You don't even need to care about what happens to the manure after it leaves your horse's stall. When you board your horse, you pay for the privilege of showing up, fussing with your horse as required, and going home.

Additionally, if you choose full or partial board, you pay for the convenience of having feed, bedding, and care of your horse arranged by someone else. This is particularly helpful for those who have very busy or irregular schedules. When you board your horse under one of these arrangements, you don't have to worry about showing up at the barn at 6am on the dot to give your horse his food. You don't have to experience gut-crushing guilt at having to skip a day of mucking his stall. Boarding removes all of the stress of coordinating suppliers, brainstorming creative solutions, and finding the right amount of time to get everything accomplished.

Boarding at some facilities can take a lot of stress out of the horse ownership experience including the vet and farrier care aspect. Many larger facilities have a standing contract with a certain vet practice and local farrier, which means you simply need to contact the barn owner or fill out a sign up sheet when your horse needs its regularly scheduled care. Additionally, in the event of an emergency, you have someone you can contact right away, instead of shopping around for professionals with emergency after-hours services.

You'll also have access to more resources than you might at home. While building and maintaining your own riding area can be expensive and time-consuming, boarding your horse at a barn that already has this considered removes all of that stress. Some barns offer a variety of amenities that horse owners can take advantage of, including indoor and outdoor riding arenas, jumps, barrels, round pens, and trails.

You'll also likely find some very cool bonuses at bigger boarding facilities such as heated tack rooms, wash racks with hot and cold water, view rooms, indoor bathrooms for riders, access to a trailer, onsite horse shows, and more. Some barns are incredibly luxurious with full kitchens, lounge rooms with fireplaces and sofas, and therapeutic massage specialists to attend to your horse each day. Others can only promise you a safe stall and reasonable pasture access. We'll take a look at how to make the right choice for your budget and horse in the next chapter.

Lastly, if you're the type of person who enjoys spontaneously joining coworkers for happy hour, heading out for a romantic weekend getaway, or planning a month-long work vacation to explore South America, boarding your horse offers much more flexibility. In full and partial care situations, you'll just need to let your barn owner know if you're going on an extended holiday. Even in self-care and pasture board situations, you may have some wiggle room in which the barn owner will help out with daily chores for a temporary period at an additional charge.

Disadvantages of Boarding Your Horse

There are, of course, a few downsides to boarding. The first- and most undeniable-concern for many owners is the cost. Depending on where you live, the size of the facility, and the services included, your board costs may run several hundreds or even thousands of dollars each month for each horse. This is the price of convenience.

Most of the time, the cost makes perfect sense. Add up everything you buy for your horse over the course of a month, and you might be shocked at the monthly total. Paying for what you need as you need it may make more sense for your budget than dropping a cool $1,000 at the start of every month. Remember, too, that you're paying for the maintenance of the facility and any fun extras that are included with your board such as bedding or a regular feeding schedule.

Many barn owners live onsite, meaning their home is somewhere on the same property as the barn. This can be great if you want the peace of mind that comes with knowing that if there's an emergency, someone is on hand. Conversely, many barn owners ask that their boarders respect set barn hours. This means you can't run out for a quick midnight ride on your horse without permission. This makes sense, of course, because no one likes to be awoken in the middle of the night by surprise guests, even if they do have a legitimate purpose for being on your property in the middle of the night.

When you board your horse, you must relinquish at least some of the care of your horses. Nearly every barn owner will allow you to feed whatever grain your horse requires to be well, for example, but they might charge an extra storage fee for adding an extra bin to the feed room. You may have to accept that your horse will be turned out when the staff has time to turn him out, rather than going out to the pasture at seven on the dot. You won't have a choice about when buckets are cleaned, what type of fencing is used, or when your horse gets each meal.

This can become very stressful for some horse owners, especially those who are used to taking care of their horses in a very specific way and on a very specific schedule. You will need to make sure both you and your horse are okay with other people handling them, feeding them, and cleaning their stall. If you want to add rubber mats to the floor of your horse's stall, or you don't want them to go outside when the weather forecast is unfavorable, you'll have to coordinate with your barn owner instead of just taking care of it yourself.

At the same time, you'll have more people around. This can be both good and bad, depending on your preferences and the individuals involved. There is something very special about the friendships that can be forged between like-minded horse people. Having someone to help you work through various issues with your horse as your "eyes on the ground" can be incredibly helpful, even if you're working with a professional trainer. Meeting up for trail rides or riding together can bring a new level of excitement to each event. Plus, it's great to have someone you can confide in who understands exactly what challenges and concerns you have regarding your horse.

On the flip side, sharing your space and resources with multiple people can be frustrating. You may arrive at the barn without a minute to spare, only to find that someone else is using the arena. There will always be at least one person who will leave their equipment set up, meaning you'll always have to clean up after them. Equestrians often have very strong opinions about horse care, which means there is eternally some type of gossip or drama amongst boarders. You may come to the barn expecting peace and quiet to enjoy your horse, only to find the barn absolutely buzzing with other boarders doing various things, none of which may be conducive to the solace and serenity you were seeking.

This means you may have a certain sense of pressure to fit in. It is important to remember that you are here for your horse and not to make other people happy. As long as your horse is healthy and happy, you should feel good about yourself. Still, that can be difficult when other people in your barn subject you to a constant barrage of suggestions and criticism. Bear in mind that not every barn will have excessive amounts of drama or cliques. You'll get a feel for who the other boarders are and what is expected of you as a boarder when you tour the facility.

Author's Anecdote: What to Do When You're the Horse of a Different Color

Years ago, I kept Red at a large private facility. The owners had once had a large breeding and showing program but had retired. As a result, they had dozens of empty stalls, a huge indoor arena, an outdoor arena with amazing footing, a well-kept series of trails, and gorgeous pastures. I was introduced to them through a mutual friend, and they agreed that three of us could keep our horses on their property under a self-care arrangement.

I lived more than an hour away from the facility, but the three of us took turns taking care of each other's horses, which made it easier for me. Since they lived closer, they took morning care shifts, and I cleaned stalls and fed in the evenings.

We got along very well with the facility owners, and after some time, they agreed to help us out with things like supplying bedding and turning out our horses for us. It was absolutely ideal for Red and I... until it wasn't.

A well-known local trainer began leasing the facility. She asked the three of us if we would like to leave and seemed surprised when we declined. After all, we'd been there first! Still, the facility was enormous, and I naively figured there was room for all of us.

I was very wrong. Some days, I would find the arena filled with up to ten riders at a time, none of whom were very competent at steering their horses. We were asked to sign an agreement that we could not have other trainers at the facility; only the trainer who was leasing the facility was permitted to give lessons. Even though she and I did not ride or compete in the same discipline, she was adamant that my dressage trainer could not teach on the premises.

Eventually, I was "banished" to the former stud barn. This barn was actually ideal for me because it was a detached structure on the other side of the property. I had a private stall for Red and my own tack room for all of my stuff. He had a giant stall, private paddock, and a giant pasture, which he shared with the yearlings during the day. The downside to this arrangement was that the driveway would flood or ice over during inclement weather, which meant there were days I couldn't get to Red's barn in my car. I started riding Red in the pasture or on the trails instead of in the arena because we couldn't access it.

The trainer asked me every month when I was going to leave because she needed my stall for paying students. I assumed that by sticking to myself, not getting in the way, and keeping everything clean and in good condition, I would be fine. Instead, the trainer and her students became increasingly aggressive in reminding me that I didn't fit in. I didn't ride their discipline, my horse wasn't their preferred breed, and I didn't have a show record to speak of. None of these things were important to me, but they were important to them.

Not every boarding experience will be unpleasant. I currently board my horses in an absolute paradise. All of the riders are the same age and experience level as I am. None of our horses are the same breed. Each boarder has been with our trainer for many years.

We aren't in it for the ribbons; we're in it because we love our horses and cherish our experiences with them. We bond over the simple things like finding a great deal on winter blankets. We share many similarities such as an appreciation for classical music and historical fiction. We're no less of a team just because we don't go to shows.

The moral of this story is that not every boarding experience is going to be the same. It is absolutely vital to visit every boarding facility that interests you to get a feel of the environment and vibe. Talk to the other boarders. Meet their horses. What types of disciplines are ridden? Can outside trainers teach on the property? Does the facility host onsite competitions, clinics, or camps? What provisions do they offer for boarders who prefer not to participate in those activities? What types of riders are at the facility-- professionals, adult amateurs, juniors, or are the riders mostly casually interested in having fun with their horses?

It is possible to get along with a horse of a different color, but many boarders find that life is a lot more peaceful when they board with like-minded individuals. Red and I learned a lot from our experience at that facility-- specifically, what type of environment we don't enjoy. I recommend boarders caught in similar situations always take the high road, and remember there are always people like you out there. They may not be at the same barn right now, but they are out there. Keep your head high and seek out better options.

Chapter 3: Things to Ask Yourself When Deciding to Build or Board

There have been a lot of concepts thrown around in the past two chapters, and your head may be spinning with "if-then" concepts and trying to juggle many different possibilities at the same time.

Deciding whether you want to build your own facility to keep your horse at home versus paying to board your horse on another person's property truly can be confusing, emotional, and frustrating. Therefore, this chapter is intended to outline the questions you need to ask yourself before you make your final decision.

If you decide to board your horse, there will also be another myriad of questions you may potentially ask. Those questions tend to stray a bit from the intended purpose of this particular list, but as they are no less important. I have added them within the Resources section. For the time being, however, we'll focus on making the first big decision: to keep your horse at home or board them.

Let's start with your budget:
- How much will it cost to build a safe and comfortable home for your horse?
- What insurance considerations and expenses would you incur housing a horse at your home?
- Do you prefer to pay a set amount for all of your expenses each month, or take care of expenses as they occur?
- Do you have adequate savings to cover an unexpected situation like repairing a fence line or stall?

Next, let's look at your time constraints:
- Are you able and willing to be available to your horse around the clock?

- Can you adhere to a strict daily routine of feeding, cleaning up after, and attending to your horse's needs?
- Is traveling or living spontaneously important to you?
- Alternatively, do you have someone reliable who can help you care for your horse when you are otherwise occupied?

Now, consider your overall enthusiasm about the following tasks. Remember you will be doing these chores in every type of weather applicable to your location:

- Daily stall cleaning-- removing several pounds of manure and replacing soiled bedding
- Lifting, stacking, and separating hay
- Dumping, scrubbing, and refilling water buckets
- Checking every inch of fencing

Can you provide the following resources to help keep your horse comfortable and healthy?

- Water source
- Electricity
- Manure management system
- Pasture rotation strategy

Last, but certainly not least, take a minute to consider your horse's preferences:

- Does your horse require a lot of time outside to maintain their sanity, or do they hate turnout?
- Does your horse enjoy being in a herd environment, or do they prefer to be less social?
- Does your horse have a hard time adjusting to new environments?
- Does your horse require specialized care that would be unavailable either at home or while boarding?

When considering these questions, bear in mind that there are no wrong answers. As long as you keep your horse's health and wellness as the primary consideration in answering these questions, you are doing the right thing.

It might surprise you to learn that some horse owners who have a facility at their home often decide to temporarily board their horses. There are many reasons why they might decide to do this including taking advantage of the seasonal amenities such as a heated barn in the winter or a fantastic trail system in warm weather. They may also want to take advantage of daily training with a professional, or may board only when the horse or human is recovering from an injury or illness, or during construction/ maintenance/updates to the home barn.

When you make the decision to keep your horse at home or board him, you're not required to stick with your decision forever. As long as you have access to a trailer or hauling service, you can move your horse as much as your budget and his tolerance for trailer rides and routine disruptions permits.

These are not easy questions to answer. There will obviously be days when you don't feel like getting out of bed before the sun. You'll sweat, freeze, and be frustrated and uncomfortable. However, in order to provide the best possible lifestyle for your horse, you need to be honest with yourself: is this something you are willing to do, or is it best left to the professionals? Your horse will thank you just as much for your honesty as he will for the care that allows him to thrive.

SECTION 4: PREPARING TO CARE FOR A HORSE

So far, we've taken a look at the considerations of having a horse, including what they'll need to be happy and healthy, along with what a perfect home for a horse would include. We've discussed whether it would make more sense for you, your horse, your budget, and your capabilities to keep that horse at home, or board it at another facility. We've also examined some of the major pros and cons of each option.

Compared to the number of variables and potential decisions to be made in the previous sections, this section is "easy." At this point, you've found the ideal horse, you've got a solid grasp on the various aspects of horse care, and you know where your horse is going to live. Now you just need to get that space ready for your horse's arrival and prepare for the first few days, weeks, and months following your horse's entrance into your life.

The days leading up to -- and even a few days following -- your horse's arrival may be very stressful. The intent of this section is to help you gain footing on what needs to be done and how to get it accomplished. There are a lot of moving parts as you organize for transport, so it's important to stay focused so you can complete each step along the way.

Once it's all over and your horse is relaxing contentedly, you'll have a much clearer picture of the amazing relationship you're about to forge with this very fascinating creature. But in the meantime, it's going to be a lot of finding, organizing, cleaning, signing, and planning.

Author's Anecdote: Horse Owners Are Very Stable People

I've had the pleasure of having numerous equine companions. Each time, the experience was a little different. When I bought my first horse, his previous owner threw in all of his equipment from the open bag of treats to his custom-fit saddle. I didn't need to pay for anything but the horse himself and the first month of board.

Red was a spontaneous purchase. He was in such terrible condition that I wasn't sure what I would need, so I showed up with a halter and lead rope and headed to the tack shop afterwards. Each horse that I've rescued has been somewhat spontaneous and needs-based, so I generally have little time to prepare. But one horse stands out as being the purchase I was least prepared to make.

I had seen a horse online that struck a note with me. I wasn't sure why, but there was something very special about this horse. I conversed with his current owner via the sales site, and I got a feel for what was going on. She no longer had the resources to continue to care for him, and he needed a new home by the end of the month. To complicate matters, she shared this detail with me just two weeks before the month was ending.

I was out of the state at the time, and I was unable to leave my current location in time to bring this horse home. My trainer was happy to provide a stall for him, but I coordinated his trial ride, purchase, transport, Coggins, and initial health examination all via email or phone. It's commonly said that you should never buy a horse sight-unseen, and I agree wholeheartedly, which is why I relied on a trusted equine professional to evaluate and provide her own review of the horse before I made the purchase.

Thankfully, everything went off like clockwork. Everyone was on time and courteous, and my horse made it home right on schedule. I was very excited to meet him for the first time a few days later. He's currently making a splash in the eventing world and having the time of his life.

I wouldn't recommend this process to anyone who hasn't completed the process several times before. It's important to make sure everyone communicates and that you're thoroughly prepared to be present for as many steps in the process as possible. Someone could have swapped out the horse I bought for another horse. The transporter could have been less honest about the time frame of travel or the costs. Both barn owners needed to be present to sign off on the transport as well. Meanwhile, I was glued to my phone trying to make sure every step went smoothly.

I highly encourage you to get everything ready ahead of time. Buy all of the supplies you need or think you might need. Contact all of the professionals you'll want on your team. Plan out your routines, and get an idea of what your horse is going to need from the moment he steps off the trailer going forward. Sure, there will be bumps in the road and last minute changes, but having clear expectations will make adjusting to the "horse life" that much easier.

Chapter 1: Things You'll Need before Your Horse Arrives

Some people love shopping while other people would rather participate in any other activity. Therefore, it is either very good news or very bad news that you will need to go shopping before your horse arrives at your home or at its new boarding facility.

The good news is that there are many places to source the items you'll need. Feed and farm equipment stores, such as Tractor Supply Company or Rural King, will often have all of the required items, along with a few extras that your horse may appreciate. If you have a nearby feed mill or tack shop, these are also great places to find what you and your new buddy will need.

Online shopping is also a wonderful option. Many online equine retailers offer free shipping for orders over a certain amount, which can be helpful when you're shipping several hundred or even thousands of dollars in supplies at once. Most carry an amazing array of products, from a package of eye hooks that can support the weight of a ten gallon water bucket, to a brand new show saddle.

Of course, it's easy to get carried away when it comes to shopping for your horse. Monogrammed saddle pads, coolers, and winter blankets may leap out at you from the web pages as you scroll. Equestrians have a tradition of color-coordinating all of their horses' clothing, from bell boots and polo wraps to the rhinestones in the browband of their bridles, so you may be blown away by the sheer volume of options you have.

For the most part, the least expensive options will be sufficient for a first time horse owner. While the differences in quality between a $20 halter and a $120 halter will be obvious to you, they really aren't that important to the horse. When shopping, look for products that are safe and durable. You can always buy what you need now and save up to splurge on more expensive products you desire later.

There are a few places where you should not compromise, however. Brand new saddles that retail under $200, for example, should be thoroughly examined before you spend your money. Many of these are constructed of poor quality leather that rips easily. Additionally, the interior construction of the saddle may not be very durable. Often, these saddles start leaking padding or the tree which supports the rider's body will crack.

On the flip side, the internet is a great place to find used and consignment tack and equipment. Sites like eBay and Facebook Marketplace are great places to find amazing deals on horse equipment. Nearly every equestrian will tell you of an enviable purchase they made through sites such as these, and the good deals aren't hard to find if you know what you're looking for. Sometimes national retailers such as SmartPak, Dover, Chick's, and State Line Tack will sell their floor samples which can be another way to get great deals on slightly used high quality equipment.

Local tack swaps and sales are another way to find necessities at a fraction of the price. Often, these events will be hosted by a local 4-H group or riding club, so stay tuned to your local events calendar to find a tack swap near you.

So what types of equipment do you need to have on hand prior to your horse's arrival? I recommend having the following items at a bare minimum:

Equipment for Feeding and Watering Your Horse:
One plastic 8 quart bucket for water
One plastic bucket or rubber pan for feed
One three quart feed scoop
A heavy duty hose
Rubber or metal stock tank to serve as a water trough in the pasture
Dish soap and toilet brush for cleaning buckets

Exceptions: Some stalls have built-in feed dishes and/or automatic waterers. In this case, you may wish to have a spare bucket on hand in case the power goes out or for soaking injuries, but it isn't an immediate requirement. Additionally, those who choose to board their horse may not need to provide these items if they're already installed.

Equipment for Handling Your Horse:

One halter

One lead rope

One lunge line

Note: Halters can be made of many materials including nylon, rope, and leather. Some barns require horses to wear "breakaway" halters as a safety measure. These are halters with a leather crown piece that is designed to snap if your horse gets caught on something. Don't worry- you can purchase additional crown pieces so you can keep using the same halter. All leather halters will function in the same way, but full nylon and rope halters will not yield in the event of a struggle.

Equipment for Mucking Stalls:

A wheelbarrow or wheeled hand cart for muck buckets

One plastic manure fork

One rake or metal-tine fork

A heavy duty shovel

Note: The bigger the wheelbarrow the more you can pull out of your horse's stall at once, but the heavier it will be. Make sure you can safely handle your stall mucking equipment when it's full to avoid making a stinky mess in the barnyard.

Equipment for Grooming:

One rubber curry comb

One rubber grooming mitt

One soft body brush

One stiff body brush

One hoof pick

One hoof brush

One heavy duty comb for mane and tail

Fly spray

Equine shampoo

Conditioner for the mane and tail

Baby oil

Several towels

Note: Shampoo, conditioner, and baby oil may seem unnecessary if you're not planning to show your horse. However, all three of these products will come in very handy for horses that spend a lot of time outside. They easily remove caked on dirt and mud. Baby oil is particularly helpful for removing burrs, thistles, and thorns from manes and tails without damaging the hair.

First Aid Kit:

Multiple rolls of 4-inch self-adhesive bandage tape (such as Vetrap or Vet Flex)

One set of standing wraps

One roll of cotton wool

Multiple rolls of gauze

Petroleum jelly

Thermometer with retrieval clip

Sanitary pads or baby diapers (great for placing medication or pressure on wounds!)

Rubber gloves

Duct tape

A tube of Banamine*

A tube of Bute*

Epsom salts or Epsom paste

Antiseptic wound cream

may require vet approval for purchase; pay attention to storage requirements

Note: There are several other topical wound treatments that you may need to add such as Fura-zone, Betadine, Swat, or Wonder Dust. These are very helpful treatments to have on hand for various stages of wound treatment that may not be necessary in an emergency situation. Invest in these products as you can-- they typically have a long shelf life if stored correctly.

Storage Solutions:

One heavy duty sealable, moisture-proof container per type of grain/supplement

One sealable, moisture-proof container for the first aid kit

Hooks for hanging up halters/lead ropes/lunge lines that are not in use

Racks or bins for storing clean blankets (one per blanket)

Note: As mentioned earlier, grain cannot be stored in its bag as the bag is generally not moisture proof. Additionally, wildlife, insects, and the horses themselves will be very interested in having access to all of your feed components. This is why heavy-duty, sealable containers are recommended. Examples include pest-proof garbage cans, lockable plastic trunks, or metal containers that can be latched. Some people repur-pose old chest freezers to hold their various animal feeds. You can also find bins and containers specifically designed for livestock feed.

In addition to these very necessary items, there are many items that will be helpful for both you and your horse. I consider these items "optional" because they may or may not be necessary depending on your location, whether you board or not, and your current and future plans for your horse. These include:

- Heavy duty stall fans
- Horse-formulated salt and mineral blocks
- Heated water buckets
- Ladder or step stool
- Fly predators
- Tack, including:
  - Saddle
  - Bridle
  - Bit
  - Reins
  - Saddle pad
  - Girth or cinch

A Word about Blankets

I'd also like to take a moment to speak briefly about blankets and blanketing. The topic is so extensive and passionately discussed that it could be a separate book altogether. However, as a person new to horse care, you'll want to know the basics.

There are many different types of horse blankets, and your horse may require all of them or none at all. Your horse may come with his own full wardrobe, depending on the seller. These are some of the more common blanket types you may find:

Cooler: a thin blanket designed to wick away moisture and prevent a hot and sweaty horse from getting too cold too quickly. These are generally designed to be worn for a short period of time and do not have straps or fasteners, which means you won't want to leave them on an unsupervised horse. Horses are pretty good at taking off blankets on their own and will deposit unwanted blankets on their stall floor. It's much easier and less messy for a human to remove it for them.

Stall sheet/Stable blanket: a thin blanket to provide warmth and moisture wicking to prevent overheating. These generally have adjustable straps at the belly and neck so that horses can wear them for a longer period of time without removing them. They are not waterproof or durable, however, so a horse who is turned out in a stall sheet may find creative ways to destroy it.

Rain sheet: a true rain sheet is simply a waterproof blanket which fastens at the neck and under the belly. These are often tear resistant and appropriate for turnout.

Turnout sheet: these are the most durable of horse blankets. They are waterproof and insulated. They are rated by weight, which corresponds to how much insulation they contain. A lightweight blanket contains 150 to 250 grams of fill, which is appropriate for temperatures below 40 degrees Fahrenheit. A medium to heavyweight blanket contains 250 to 300 grams of insulation, and a heavyweight blanket can range from 300 to 400 grams of filling. Many have leg straps to help them stay in place while your horse runs and plays in the field.

Combination sheet: this is a pair of blankets sold as a set. The most common combination is a medium or heavyweight stable blanket with a rain sheet. These blankets typically have extra fasteners and straps to keep them connected to each other when used as a pair though they can be used separately.

Fly sheet/Scrim: this is a very thin sheet used for protecting sensitive horses from fly bites during seasons where the pests are at their worst.

Blankets are sized by measuring from the center of the chest, over the shoulder and belly, and to the point of the rump under the tail. A horse who measures 72 inches from chest to rump will wear a size 72 blanket, for example.

Blankets can cause chafing if they're too tight or are worn for a long period of time. Sleazys, slinkys, and slickers are all names of Lycra products that can be slipped over a horse's head and under a blanket to alleviate chafing. These types of hoods are also used to keep horses clean and well-groomed before a show. They look a bit silly at first glance, but they can be very helpful in avoiding painful blanket rubs. They are also not always waterproof, so you may want to double check that fact before turning your horse out in the snow, rain, or mud.

In warm weather, you may want to provide your horse with a fly mask as well. Insects love horses, but horses do not return the sentiment. You may be surprised at the number of insects that will buzz around your horse's face. A fly mask is a type of mesh covering that wraps around a horse's face. They are available in almost infinite styles and colors and patterns, including pull-on, Velcro-fastened, over-the-ear, without ears, padded, and so on. If your horse is being bothered by bugs, a fly mask is a great investment.

Some horses have sensitive coats and skin and require a variety of different blankets. Some require none at all. Pay attention to whether your horse appears to be uncomfortable or too cold, with signs such as shivering, pawing, a tucked tail, or even refusing to drink water. Feel their ears and chest. If they feel cold to the touch, this can also indicate that your horse may be chilly.

At the same time, remember that most horses grow a winter coat to help them stay warm. Unless you clip your horse to keep him from overheating in his naturally created winter coat, he should be pretty good at moderating his own body heat in a variety of temperatures. There are, of course, exceptions to this theory, so always put eyes and hands on your horse to make sure he's comfortable.

Keep in mind also that these are just some very basic guidelines for what you'll want to have on hand. Over time, you will most assuredly acquire a number of items that are a little more "want" than "need." Horse owners are often accused of "hoarding" equipment. There may be a little truth to that, but the fact is that multiples of some items are more than warranted. Saddle pads, for example, get sweaty and dirty quickly, and often require air drying. Therefore, having several on hand is not a bad idea. Another example is the manure fork. Despite our best efforts, these do break and bend, and given their purpose in the barn, must be replaced immediately. Having a backup fork is good planning. Multiple manure buckets or wheelbarrows can also be helpful, especially if you have several stalls or a long haul to the manure pile.

Of course, you may choose to add and delete from these suggestions as necessary, depending on your situation. If you are boarding your horse, you may be required to use a certain type of feed storage solution, and you likely won't need to supply your own hose, for example. Always double-check with the barn owner as to what equipment you are expected to bring. This and other questions are addressed in the "Questions to Ask a Prospective Boarding Barn" portion of the Resources section.

Chapter 2: Moving a Horse Into a New Space

Bringing a horse home for the first time can bring about many emotions. It's very exciting, of course, but it can also be cause for great anxiety, especially if this is your very first time adding a horse to your life. There are a few things you can do in preparation of the big day that will help things move along more smoothly.

The first thing to work out is how your horse is going to get from wherever it is now to its new home and whether that home is going to be on your own property or at a boarding facility. After all, it's not like you can just ride a horse down the interstate!

If you do not already own a trailer or have one at your disposal, you will need to arrange a trailer to pick up and deliver your horse. Years ago, I was lucky enough to have a barn owner who had her stock trailer constantly hitched to a capable dually truck. I just needed to text her to tell her when I needed it and where I was taking it. I had to have a copy of my insurance information on file with the office, and I was expected to return it with a full tank of gas. Today, however, I don't have that luxury, which means relying on friends or horse shipping services as necessary.

No matter where you source your trailer, there are a few things you need to keep in mind. First, ask what type of trailer it is. Ramp trailers have a built-in ramp that lowers to allow the horse to easily walk up into the trailer. Step-up trailers are named because there is no ramp, and your horse will literally have to step up into the body of the trailer.

A stock trailer is big and spacious, as it's designed to accommodate a variety of livestock. Some horses actually prefer these trailers since they don't feel overly cramped or confined. Trailers designed specifically for horses often have permanent dividers that help encourage the horse to stay standing. A small window will help keep air moving through the trailer during transit. Always remember to shut the window or put up the screen guard before you start driving. Letting your horse hang his head out the window while zooming down the freeway is incredibly dangerous.

Of course, if you're buying a horse from another state or region, you may not be there in person to load your horse and make the journey home with him. If you are using a shipping service, or hiring someone to bring your horse to you, make sure you ask how often they will stop for hay and water. If the trip is very long, where will they be overnighting? Will your horse have the opportunity to get out of the trailer to stretch his legs?

Travelling via trailer isn't exactly easy for horses since they need to stand and balance in the trailer for the duration of the trip. Your horse may come off the trailer a bit lethargic and possibly even a bit dehydrated, depending on the length of the trip. Conversely, he might be very excited to meet everyone in his new home and bounce off the trailer merrily while loudly announcing his arrival to anyone in earshot. Be prepared for either response, and consider parking the trailer in a spot where you can easily shuttle the horse into his stall or a safe paddock after unloading.

Before your horse comes home, you should request any medical paperwork you need, such as a health certificate or Coggins test result. You also have the right to ask about any prior reports, such as x-rays or reports following a major injury or illness. At the very least, try to get the dates the horse was last dewormed, along with the dewormer they received. Also ask about vaccinations-- when did they receive them, and which ones were they given?

This is important to ensure your horse is starting off his new life with you on a healthy note. Deworming is necessary to flush the horse's system of any intestinal parasites which shed through passing manure. Some parasites are normal since horses often eat in the same area where manure is passed. However, not all dewormers are the same. Some deworming products are relatively gentle, while others must be given at precise dosages for the horse's safety. It's important to know which your horse has received, and how recently, to avoid intestinal upset.

You'll also want to speak with the previous owner about any stall vices your horse may come with. The term "stall vices" sounds a lot worse than it is, but many of these can be very concerning for a first-time horse owner. As noted in the beginning of this book, not all horses are necessarily thrilled about spending the day in a stall, so some of them develop bad habits as an outlet for their energy and emotions.

Cribbing is considered one of the most "unforgivable" stall vices because it is a very hard habit to control, and can cause significant damage to your horse and their habitat. A horse who cribs will latch his teeth onto a solid surface, usually a piece of fencing, a gate, or a ledge in his stall, and suck air through his mouth. When the horse does this, it releases endorphins, so the horse becomes more or less physically addicted to the practice. It not only makes a really annoying "HRUNK" noise, but can lead to the development of ulcers in the horse, and can lead to damage of the surfaces he uses to crib on. Horses don't enjoy the action so much as the flood of endorphins, but many will crib relentlessly until the habit is under control.

The good news is that there are many types of cribbing collars available through equine retailers. These simply buckle around a horse's neck at the jaw and allow the horse to eat and breathe naturally. When the horse attempts to suck air after latching to a solid surface, the collar will not allow them to inflate their windpipe. A grazing muzzle is also a good choice for a cribbing horse. There are some commercially available pastes and bad-tasting goos that can be applied to surfaces to dissuade cribbing as well, but a really enthusiastic cribber will find a way to work around these.

Wood chewing is a similar issue, though harder to control. A horse who chews wood is often more bored than hungry, though supplying loads of hay can often keep them occupied. Stall toys are one way to keep a horse from becoming too bored, along with regular exercise and turnout. A wood chewer may need to wear a grazing muzzle in a boarding barn to keep him from gnawing his entire stall down. Splinters in the mouth, esophagus, stomach, and intestine can be very dangerous, in addition to the inconvenience of eating holes in his habitat, so wood chewing should be controlled and limited as quickly as possible.

Weaving and stall walking are similar habits in that they involve hyper activity within the stall. Horses who weave stand still and sway from side to side. Stall walkers, on the other hand, obsessively trudge in circles in their stalls. Neither of these is particularly dangerous for the horse, but your horse will go through bedding much more quickly than one who spends more time standing still.

The number one way to deal with these stall vices is through exercise and turnout. Each of these is a clear sign that the horse is stressed out in his stall, so spending constructive time outside of the stall will help relieve that stress. That's not always practical, however. This is why it's a good idea to ask the previous owner about any stall vices before your horse arrives. The previous owner can tell you what to expect, how they've dealt with it in the past, and make any recommendations going forward.

Once your horse is in his new home, you'll want to be cautious about introducing him to other horses. Though horses are by nature very social creatures, some of them don't make a great first impression, especially when they're already excited or stressed out from a trailer ride. On the other hand, some horses will go to great trouble to join the herd as quickly as possible by hopping the fence, or unlatching their stall door to meet their new friends.

Horses meeting each other for the first time typically make a lot of strange noises. There may be pawing, kicking, rearing, and striking at each other. Many experts recommend introducing horses through a safe barrier, such as the front of a stall. Meeting through the fence is pretty common also, but it's important to monitor them during the process, as a flailing hoof can easily get stuck in the fence. Bites and kicks are normal, but it's important to assess any damages immediately. Tiny nicks and bruises should heal naturally, but giant bite wounds and lacerations will require immediate vet attention.

There is honestly no way to accurately predict how horses are going to react to new friends and neighbors. Red, for example, has been turned out with other geldings, mares, foals, and stallions with equal success; however, he will chase any grey or light colored horse. As a thoroughbred, he has both the speed and endurance to run the poor pony ragged, so ideally, he's only turned out with darker horses. On the other hand, he loves miniature horses and will protect them from any more aggressive horse who might try to bully them. I can't explain it, but I do my best to accommodate his preferences for everyone's safety.

Over time, you'll learn more about your horse, including his likes, dislikes, and preferences. The first 24 hours are a critical time for building this understanding, as well as developing a relationship. While it's certainly not always practical to camp out in your new buddy's stall for a full day, there are a few things you'll want to pay attention to over the course of the first few hours and days. Here are a few specific things to note as you get to know your equine companion:

- When does he drink the most water? Many horses drink throughout the day, but some horses will guzzle their water right after feeding.
- Does he eat his hay enthusiastically, or pick at it? If he leaves his hay, does he finish it eventually, or throw it out of his stall/urinate on it/stuff it in his water bucket?
- Where does he choose to urinate/leave manure? Some horses prefer to keep their waste in a specific corner of the stall, while others just don't seem to care.
- How often does he produce manure? Is it solid or loose? Some horses will have loose stool after a stressful event like moving, but it should stabilize within a day.
- Does he enjoy rolling in his stall? Horses love to roll in fresh shavings, mud, and dirt, but it can be easy for a horse to get cast in his stall, meaning he wedges himself up against the wall and can't flip over. When this happens, humans need to help them reposition themselves to get up.
- Does he have good stall manners, or does he pin his ears or snap at other horses and people as they walk past his stall?

These are just a few good notes to have in mind going forward with your new horse. You want to get a baseline understanding of your horse, so you can know when they're acting strangely, as unusual behavior can be a sign of health problems. You may also wish to take your horse's temperature, so you know what "normal" looks like in your horse.

With this said, understand that your horse is a living being, and may vary his routine from time to time. However, if your horse normally drinks an entire bucket of water in the evening, but in the morning his water is completely untouched, this could indicate a problem. A horse who normally doesn't roll in his stall who is suddenly lying down and doesn't want to get up could be displaying symptoms of several issues. You need to get an idea of your horse's normal range of behaviors so that you can identify abrupt changes that may be indicative of a serious issue.

Chapter 3: Establishing Your Routine

One way in which you can start to get a feel for what your horse's "normal" is, is by establishing your horse care routine. This will help you track any changes as the days go by as well as provide a steady schedule for your horse. Horses definitely learn to appreciate repetition. Much like any other animal, ourselves included, they can be trained to expect meals and activities at a certain time.

If you choose a full board situation for your horse, you won't necessarily need to create a routine so much as learn the order of operations for that particular facility. It's generally good etiquette to not show up in the middle of feeding time and expect to ride without clearing it with the barn owner, for example. Not only do you risk getting in the way and interrupting whatever process is going on, but your horse might be miffed about having to miss a meal.

For those who do keep their horses at home, establishing your routine is going to require some trial and error at first. You'll want to give yourself a comfortable time cushion before you have to be anywhere, in case the unexpected happens. The "unexpected" could range from a horse coming in from the field with a wound, to a water bucket breaking and requiring immediate replacement. This type of thing will almost always happen when you're rushing because you need to be somewhere, so plan ahead to give yourself some extra time.

Most horses who live in stalls enjoy at least two feedings a day consisting of hay, grain, and water. You'll want to choose the amounts you serve based on your horse's body condition and needs, as discussed earlier, which means you may want to keep hay in front of your horse's face any time he's not turned out in the field. On the other hand, if he's the type to waste his hay, you may want to dole it out just a little bit at a time, so it doesn't end up trampled and covered in manure.

You'll want to check your horse's water source several times a day to make sure that he has enough to drink and that it's clean and fresh, and he hasn't done something to make it gross. Be sure to dump and scrub water buckets regularly.

If your own schedule permits, consider cleaning your horse's stall while he's turned out in the pasture. This way, you can take your time and thoroughly clean up any manure and urine in the stall.

Some horses are impeccable housekeepers. They'll deposit their manure in one corner and urinate in one spot exclusively. These stalls are lovely to clean because you simply take out the bad and put in clean bedding.

Then you have horses who are very active in their stalls and manage to make it look like their stall hasn't been cleaned within an hour of stripping it to the floorboards and refilling it with clean bedding. I have had several horses like this-- at one point, a partial care barn owner took me aside to beg me to clean Red's stall more often. I had just cleaned it two hours prior. He had just managed to urinate in the middle and churn up the bedding into a damp, stinking mess in those two hours.

In my opinion, the best thing about stall cleaning is that, as long as you get everything dirty out and replace it with fresh bedding, there's no "right" or "wrong" way to do it. If you are new to cleaning stalls, I recommend starting with the obvious and sifting down to what's hidden. That means pulling out the piles of manure that are on top of the bedding first, then sifting through the remaining bedding to discover bedding that's soaked with urine or has been churned under a clean layer from the horse walking around, lying down, or dropping hay on top.

One popular question is, "How long does it take to clean a stall?" It really depends on the horse and how well the stall has been maintained. A horse who is a tidy keeper, who is turned out all day or all night, or who's stall is cleaned every day may just have a few piles of droppings and a single patch of urine to remove. This could take just a matter of minutes to remove. On the other hand, a horse who is on medical stall rest, who must stay in all day, may have a stall that defies reason and could require up to an hour to fully sift through.

Another common question is, "How much bedding should I put in my horse's stall?" The main goal of bedding is to absorb the moisture and smell of manure and urine, so you'll want to be sure there's enough bedding that your horse isn't trying to coexist with a giant puddle. Four to six inches of bedding is considered standard for a stall in which a horse spends a lot of time, while two to four inches may be preferred for horses who spend most of their days and nights outdoors.

Additionally, consider how much time he spends in his stall and the barn foundation. If the barn has a hard cement foundation, you might want to increase the bedding to make it more comfortable for your horse to stand on it most of the day. If you have rubber mats in your stalls, that can provide additional cushioning to make standing a little more comfortable. You will most likely need to experiment with bedding levels until you get the right amount down to a science.

As to what type of bedding you should use, the only absolute, firm, non-negotiable bedding to avoid is black walnut wood shavings. Black walnut can create an almost immediate laminitic response in horses. If you work with a local sawmill to use their discarded shavings, make sure they do not process black walnut wood.

Otherwise, there are many different types of products available. You can find very fine, dust-like shavings. These are easier to pick through with a manure fork, but tend to be so good at their job that they'll absorb ambient moisture. Some types of shavings will turn black the minute they get even a little damp. This doesn't impact their ability to do their job at absorbing the dampness and smell of manure and urine, but it does give a visual impression that the stall is not clean. Large flake shavings have a very clean look and tend to smell nice for longer, but they may be a little tricky to pick through. You may end up feeling like you're wasting a lot when you use these shavings. Newer commercially available beddings, such as pellets and corn shavings, tend to be a little pricier, but they do a very good job at reducing ammonia smells. One word of caution about pellet bedding-- always read the directions. Some need to be watered down to activate them. Until they're activated, they're round and prone to rolling when walked upon by humans. I can't count the number of times I've slipped and fallen in a stall due to pellet bedding.

Straw is also commonly used as bedding, especially in breeding barns since it doesn't stick to newborn foals' skin or get inhaled into their delicate respiratory systems. Straw is very difficult to pick through and clean, which means you may simply need to remove absolutely everything from a stall bedded with straw. It also tends to take up a lot of room on the typical manure heap. It's definitely cheap and does its job well, but cleaning a stall bedded with straw is definitely more difficult than cleaning one filled with shavings.

As you truck along, you may discover that you have more questions than you have answers. This is very common and natural in the horse world. Thankfully, we live in an age where a quick search on your smartphone should provide you with enough information to deal with the immediate consequences of your question and point you in the direction of some helpful next steps or resources.

You may need a month or so to truly establish your routine with your horse. You may discover that the way you initially set up your barn isn't as conducive to your routine as you thought, too. There truly is a lot of trial and error in horse keeping. You will make mistakes along the way. You may forget to lock up the feed at night and discover a raccoon has helped himself to as much as he could. You will tip over a full wheelbarrow in the most inconvenient spot and spend twice as long cleaning it up. Your hay will go moldy at some point. Your water pipes will freeze. You will absolutely touch the electric fence at some point and regret it. It may seem like every day you find a new problem or challenge that must be dealt with that very second.

My advice for these situations is to breathe. Stay calm so you can think clearly in the moment. It is not your horse's fault that the wheelbarrow tipped-- unless your horse pawed at it or sent it sprawling with his nose. Whenever things happen, make sure your horse is secure first. Then allow yourself whatever emotional room you need at the moment.

Every horse person has enjoyed a bad day with some weird barn problem as the cherry on top. Cry on your horse's shoulder if you need to. Scream in the tack room if you need to. You'll likely find that your horse is far more sympathetic to your pain than you might imagine. Red is a very tall horse at 16.2 hands high. I have cried on his shoulder many times over our past eleven years together. He's a very good shoulder to cry on since it's perfectly placed for me to simply lean on him, but also because he doesn't like to see humans upset. He'll turn his head and sniff at me, gently bumping me with his nose. He stands perfectly still while I get out my sadness or frustration, and then, once I've pulled myself together, he'll rub his face on my back to make me laugh.

Over time, your routine will help you turn your barn chores into more of a barn privilege, and your horse will tend to agree that this is, in fact, the best life ever.

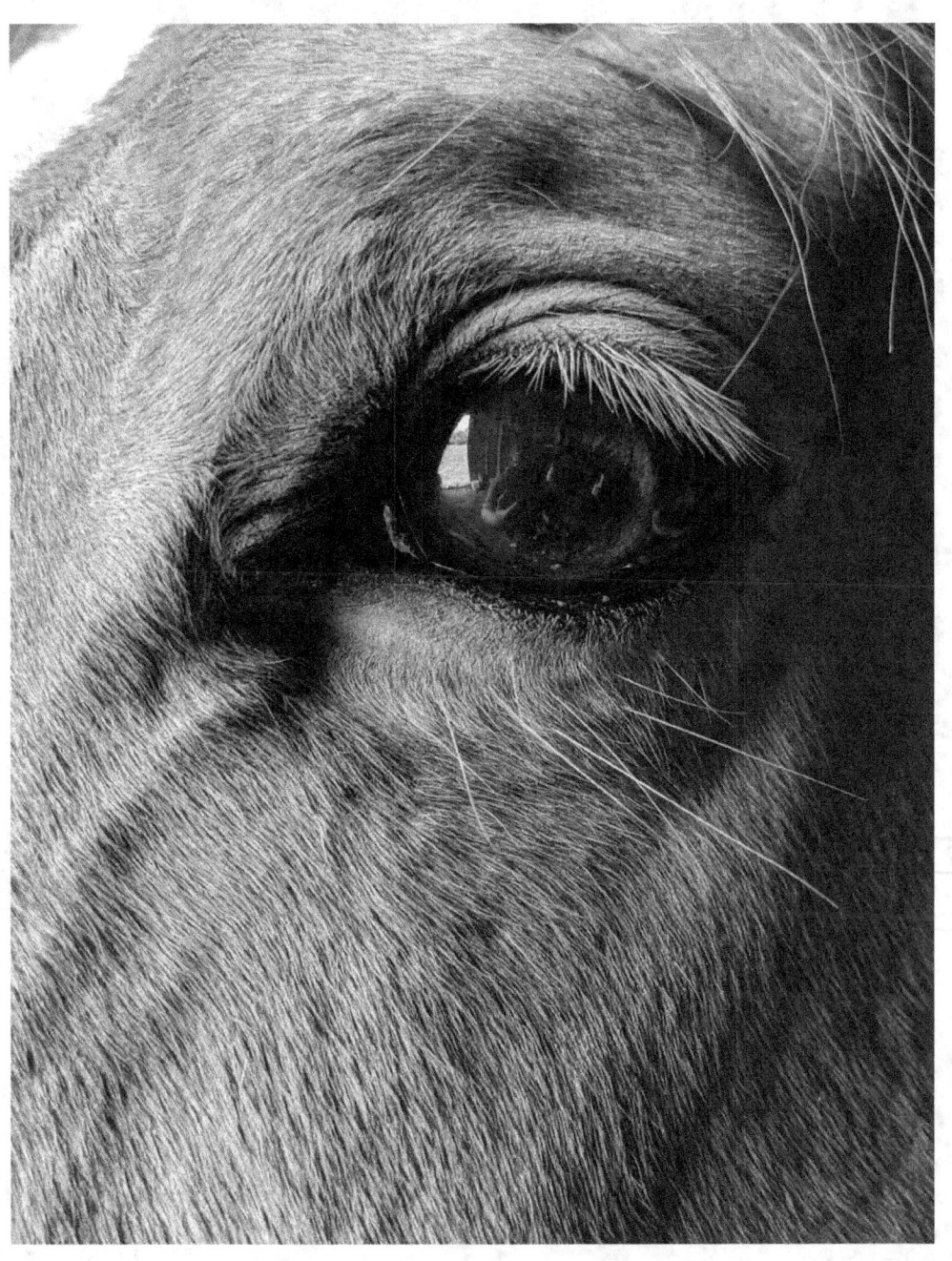

CONCLUSION

Now that you've discovered the basics of horse care, you might find yourself completely overwhelmed at how involved it can be. Not only are there a lot of moving parts, but it sounds like horses are difficult to keep alive. It sounds like long hours, heavy lifting, sweating, freezing, and a lot of money.

These assessments are true, but what in life doesn't require our blood, sweat, and tears? Car enthusiasts spend just as much time, money, and energy finding, repairing, and restoring their dream cars. Mountain climbers spend days, weeks, or months in preparation and risk their lives summiting the tallest peaks. Even the family dog requires frequent walks and potty breaks. Horses are not easy, but nothing in life truly is, especially if you love it completely.

It does take a very special kind of person to care for a horse. You have to be willing to smell strange and get dirty. You will find manure in your hair and on your face. You will need to look at some pretty gruesome wounds and ignore your disgust to take care of the oozing. You will get up earlier than you want and stay up later than you prefer. Your muscles will ache. You will miss out on some fun social activities. You may at some point "borrow" your horse's Epsom salts for your own soak.

But in return, you'll get the adoration and respect of a horse. Sure, your horse might not be as affectionate as Red, but remember-- this is a 1,000 pound beast who can run 25 miles per hour. He doesn't have to do a single thing you say unless he wants to. And over time, with proper care, he'll definitely want to. You'll hear that distinctive nicker when you come out to the barn to feed. You'll see his ears perk up when he hears your footsteps. He'll meet you at the barn door, ready to come in from turnout to spend some time with you.

Horses can't "talk" per se, in that they don't use human language to share their thoughts, but they are very honest in their actions. The deeper the bond you form with your horse, the more you'll know what's on their mind. Red, in particular, is one horse that is very clear about what he likes and doesn't like. He's tolerant of things that don't live up to his standards, but his antsy movement and caustic side-eye tell me exactly what I need to know about his opinions.

Making a horse happy will make you happy. Those quiet moments, when you're grooming your horse and suddenly hit the itchy spot, are the type that you'll cherish your entire life. You can tell all of your secrets to your horse. Your horse will listen to what a jerk your boss is, how your teachers don't understand you, or how your family is out of their minds, and he won't judge you for a single thing you say. Instead, he's more concerned that you give him water, food, medical care, and attention. And if you do all of that, and you're nice on top of that? You've made his life exponentially better.

As you've read, there's a lot to remember. I encourage everyone to come up with the reminders and resources they will need to help with each component of horse care. For example, I set a calendar reminder each week to pick up horse feed. I have supplements delivered to the barn automatically each month. I consult with my barn owner when it's time for the farrier to come out to take care of all their hooves, and I make sure I arrive on time when he comes out with cash in my hand to pay him for his services.

I personally recommend finding a mentor when starting out in horsekeeping. If you're boarding your horse, this may be your barn owner or trainer. Your 4-H equine advisor, or even a buddy you've exchanged messages with via an online forum, can provide lots of insight into common issues, or even direct you to the details you need. Horse people have a reputation for being a bit strange and overzealous, but reflecting back on the past several chapters, you may now understand why!

Over time, your daily horse care activities may become the highlight of your day. In a stressful world, it can be very enriching to take some time away from phones, computers, bosses, and email to just stand in the barn, listening to your horse quietly chomping on hay. After a hectic day of running errands and meeting deadlines, a quick, calm ride on your horse may be exactly what you need to unwind. In fact, there have been times when I simply pull a horse out of a stall and groom it from head to tail while working out some issue or complication in my non-horsey life.

Caring for a horse requires a level of discipline and dedication that you may not initially expect. People often ask me if it's "just like taking care of a giant baby," and while there are similarities, a horse is certainly more autonomous. A horse also isn't small enough to throw in a car seat or stroller for the day! When venturing into horse care, be prepared for plenty of sacrifices but appreciate the down time. Horses have instincts for a reason, and as long as you provide them with the food, water, and shelter they need, they'll be able to figure out quite a few things on their own. While domesticating an animal is a huge responsibility, it's important to remember that your horse doesn't actually need to be swaddled and tended to every minute of the day.

My hope is that this book has gotten you started on the path towards caring for your own horse. I certainly encourage you to check out the Resources section to continue researching any particular topic or area of care in which your horse may need some specialized attention. Don't consider this book the absolute encyclopedia of "Do's and Don'ts" of horsekeeping, but rather consider it more of a general text to set you on your course for learning all of the intricate details that will make your horse's particular experience much more enriching.

My wish is for you and your horse to have a long, fruitful, healthy relationship together. Whether you catch the "horse bug" and find yourself requiring at least one equine companion for the rest of your life, or only venture into horse ownership because you've found that one magical beast, I hope you enjoy the bond you form with your horse for many years to come. Yes, there will be good days and bad days, but at the end of each day, I hope that your heart will be filled with love and appreciation for that big, hairy, stinky manure machine that you've chosen to share your life with.

All the best, from my barn to yours.

RESOURCES

As horse owners, we're constantly learning and growing as science teaches us new things about our equine companions. We're constantly learning new things about equine biology, and how we, as humans, can continue to support our horses.

Neither I, nor any member of the publication team, have a direct relationship with any of the following websites or companies. None of these links are sponsored in any way, nor should you consider these links an endorsement of any kind. Rather, I've chosen these links as resources that provide usable, understandable, fact-based information about horses, horse health, and horse care.

The equestrian community is full of amazing resources. There's a lot of information to cover, so it's wonderful that so many experts and professionals post detailed articles to share the latest research and findings with the community as a whole. These resources represent just a fraction of the sites online that can provide you with all the details you may need to know about a specific horse, situation, or scenario. Don't consider this an exhaustive list by any means; instead, think of this as a starting place for continuing your quest for information.

I also recommend searching online to connect with other horse owners in your area. You might be surprised to find how many different groups and forums there may be in your state, region, or even county. These groups may share the same riding interests as you, the same breed of horse, or may simply want to gather to discuss local issues and events. These can also be great resources for finding new hay and feed sources, buying used tack and equipment, and meeting new horse enthusiast friends. For those who are very new to horses, it's a great idea to find a mentor in your area-- someone who has had horses for many years and can show you the ropes, so to speak.

Additionally, I encourage you to ask your vet if any specific questions come up about your horse's health or behavior. From helping you refine your deworming program to making recommendations on feeding, your vet has plenty of information and interest in your horse's well-being. Establishing a good working relationship with your vet can help you prevent many health conditions and help you manage any future diagnoses so you and your horse can enjoy a long, happy life together.

Lastly, I recommend getting your hands on-- and reading!-- every giant horse book you can. If you're a visual person like I am, find books that have lots of pictures which will help you decipher some of the things you see explained on the internet. These will provide you with a solid visual you can return to again and again, with the added bonus of very pretty artistic horse photos.

General Information Blogs/Publications

The following are just a smattering of the online blogs and equine publications available. Many offer both free articles as well as subscription packages. Before the internet, it wasn't uncommon for an equine professional to subscribe to at least 5 different horse magazines. Thankfully, the digital world has made it easier than ever to pick up all the greatest tips and tidbits from around the globe... though there was something very special about receiving the latest issue in the mail and obsessively reading it cover to cover!

Some of these sites also send weekly or monthly emails directly to your inbox. I personally appreciate this because it reminds me of upcoming seasonal events, like spring vaccinations or preparing for winter blanket weather. Preparation is key, and sometimes, the extra reminder is worth signing up for more emails.

https://blog.smartpakequine.com/

https://www.chronofhorse.com/

https://practicalhorsemanmag.com/

https://www.aqha.com/news-and-publications/news-and-blogs

https://dressagetoday.com/horse-health-

https://www.equisearch.com/blog

Health and Wellness

The following links will lead you to resources that specifically focus on health and wellness issues. The articles you'll find here range from general topics, such as getting your horse ready for changes in the season to very specific conditions or concerns, such as Equine Metabolic Syndrome or Anhidrosis. You may be surprised to discover how truly delicate horses are, despite being large, sturdy animals in appearance, but fear not. More and more equine health concerns can be supported by monitoring and maintenance. These resources will help you learn what to look for, what to do, and how to plan ahead.

https://www.smartpakequine.com/content/health-library

https://equinewellnessmagazine.com/

https://thehorse.com/

https://equusmagazine.com/

Equine Nutrition

Equine nutrition is a topic that is equal parts art and science. The following sites explain all of the many components of horse feed in great detail but in layman's terms. You'll be able to pick up details about your horse's specific needs from each of these websites.

Please note, though the Horse Feed Blog is sponsored by Nutrena, a brand of horse feed, it is a very comprehensive site that serves less as an advertisement for the brand and more as an equine community resource. Again, no sponsorship or affiliation exists-- I'm simply providing some of the most comprehensive resources available.

https://esc.rutgers.edu/fact_sheet/the-basics-of-equine-nutrition/
https://aaep.org/horsehealth/nutrition-key-unlocking-your-horses-health
https://www.horsefeedblog.com/about/

Just For Fun

The following links don't necessarily correspond to topics within the book, but they can help out with some side research you might be inspired to conduct after reading this book. Since we covered so much information, you may find yourself wondering "what about...". The following links are intended to help guide you down a new path of research potentially inspired by what you've read so far.

Duct Tape and Baling Twine

Seriously! It's a thing! It's definitely not recommended for permanent solutions or long-term fixes, but there are many things you can do with duct tape and baling twine to help you get through the day... so many things, in fact, that the art of repair has become something of a legend among horse people. Enjoy these articles that highlight the many ways real people have used duct tape and baling twine to help them out of some stressful situations.

https://heelsdownmag.com/the-frightening-fix-it-ways-of-horse-people/
https://www.equisearch.com/articles/uses-for-bailing-twine-16927
https://www.aqha.com/widget/-/50-horseback-riding-problems-duct-tape-can-fix

Building a Barn at Home

Again, this wasn't specifically discussed in this book, but I wanted to include some examples to help you answer the questions about budget and space required in Section 3, Chapter 3. It's difficult to appreciate how much you should budget for building and maintaining a barn, unless you have an idea of what type of structure and fence line you'd like to build.

Again, there are almost limitless resources online regarding barn plans and farm needs, so take this as a springboard for your future research, rather than an exhaustive list of options.

https://horseandrider.com/how-to/horse-barn-plans

https://equusmagazine.com/horse-care/barn_heating_ventilation_032708

https://www.horsefactbook.com/horse-care/keeping-a-horse-at-home/

Equine Equipment Retailers

For your first foray into equine ownership, you'll want to make sure you have all the right equipment. As outlined in Section 4, Chapter 1, there are quite a few things you need to have right off the bat and some things that you can wait to purchase. These are just a few of the popular US-based retailers that horse owners have trusted for decades.

Again, this book is not affiliated with any of these retailers, nor are these endorsements of the companies and their products. However, as you're getting things prepared for your horse's arrival, it's good to have a few resources for shopping and future supplies.

Author's Note: *Be sure to check out their clearance sections for hot deals and special offers!*

SmartPak: https://www.smartpakequine.com/

Dover Saddlery: https://www.doversaddlery.com/

State Line Tack: https://www.statelinetack.com/

Chick's Saddlery: https://www.chicksaddlery.com/

Valley Vet Supply: https://www.valleyvet.com/

Big Dee's: https://www.bigdweb.com/

Schneider's: https://www.sstack.com/

Questions to Ask a Prospective Boarding Barn

The first thing you'll see when you examine this list is that it is very long. This is intentional because there are many questions you'll need to ask before you move your horse into a boarding barn for the first time.

If you are moving your horse into a barn where you have taken lessons or worked for a period of time, you will likely already have the answers to some of these questions, which will help simplify the research process. However, if you are stepping into a barn for the very first time, you'll want to check this list to make sure you're organized and ready to find out everything you need to know about your horse's future habitat.

Please note that some of these questions won't be applicable for every barn. For example, a self-care barn is unlikely to have a mandatory training program and would kindly ask that you provide your own feed and bedding, which eliminates the need to ask those questions. Use your own discretion when asking these questions, and again, don't consider this an exhaustive resource. There may be regional differences in horse care needs, or requirements specific to your individual horse. However, don't be afraid to ask any question, even if it makes you feel silly. Horse people tend to be very detail-oriented, so that "silly" question might lead to information that's very important to know!

General Questions

These are basics that apply to any horse board situation. You'll want to know what's permitted, what's included, and the details that will keep your horse safe and happy as long as he's staying at that facility.

- What type of boarding do you offer?
- If this is a pasture board, do I have a stall option if my horse is ill/injured?
- If this is self-care, am I permitted to designate an alternate care taker or emergency contact?
- Would someone be able to assist my horse in an emergency?
- What is included in the monthly fee?
- When is the board due each month?
- Are there different boarding packages, and what is included in each?
- Do you offer blanket changes?
- How is the facility equipped for weather changes, such as using stall fans in the summer or heated water buckets in the winter? Is there an extra charge to take advantage of these options?
- What type of fencing do you use?
- Who takes care of the horses?
- Who will be authorized to handle my horse?
- Who performs regular maintenance?
- Does anyone live on site?
- What type of security system do they have?
- Where do riders tack up their horses?
- Where do riders exercise their horses?
- Can you ride outside of the designated arenas (such as up/down the driveway, farm perimeter, etc)?

- What is the arena footing made of, and how often is it dragged or watered?
- What type of bedding do they use, and how much is each horse allotted?
- Are there stallions on the premises?

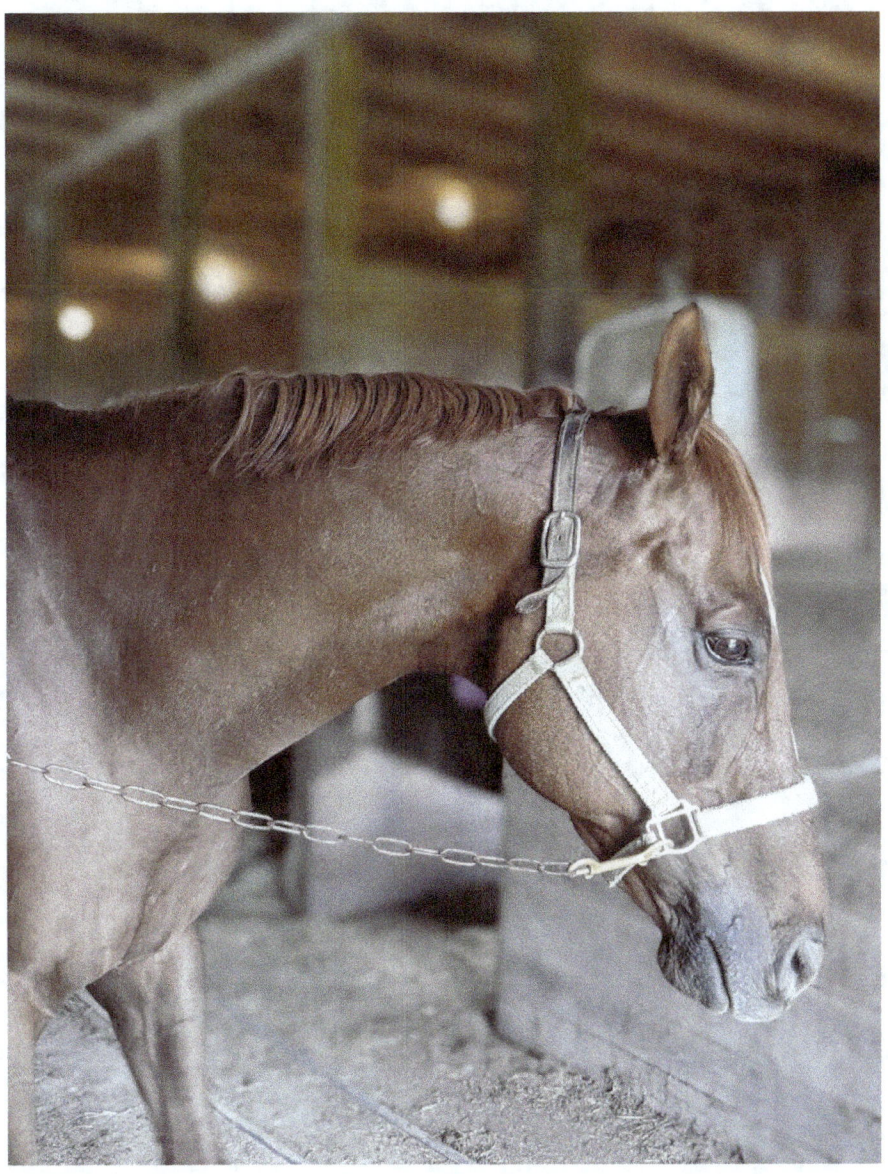

Nutritional Questions

Unless you're lucky enough to have an "air fern" horse, knowing what your horse is eating and when can be crucial to his long term health. These questions are designed to help you understand the barn's standard feeding program and any accommodations they can make for horses with special feeding needs.

- How much turnout will my horse receive?
- When are horses turned out (ex: during the day in winter, night in the summer, no turnout when it rains, etc)?
- How often are the horses fed?
- What type of grain do you feed the horses?
- Are you willing to feed grain that I provide?
- How is grain and hay stored to prevent mold or pest infestation?

Professional Assistance Questions

Everyone wants to make sure their horse lives a long, happy life. The vet, farrier, and trainer are three of the most influential people in your horse's life, besides you. Therefore, you want to make sure that your horse gets the best care possible. Since some facilities work with specific parties, you'll want to make sure you can either continue to work with your preferred providers, or that you're able to transition to the new care team easily. These questions will help you gain insight into what you'll need to do to make that happen.

- Do you have a vet and farrier that come to the barn regularly?
- How often do they come out?
- What is the process for signing up with the vet or farrier?
- May I use my own vet or farrier? Where in the barn is my vet or farrier permitted to work?
- What is your policy for veterinary care in the event of an emergency? What if I or my emergency contact is unreachable?
- Is there an onsite trainer?
- Am I required to take lessons with the onsite trainer?
- Am I permitted to receive training from an outside party?

Facility Questions

Every barn runs a little bit differently. In all of my years of experience, I've never experienced two identical facilities. Always be sure to get a complete tour of the facility, including all aisleways and arenas. Barn owners and managers should be happy to let you see and experience all the different areas of the facility, from the manure pile to where the hay is kept.

Additionally, you'll want to know about what is available for use and any procedures or policies regarding how and when it should be used. These questions will provide extra orientation around the grounds, and what to expect if you choose to move your horse there.

- What amenities are available for boarders?
- Will I need to supply my own tack trunk or lock?
- Is there a bathroom/dressing room?
- Is there running hot water?
- What hours is the barn open?
- When is the arena available?
- What is the arena etiquette (ex: yelling "door" before entering, putting equipment back or adjusting it back to height/place it was before, no riding during lessons, etc)?
- Do you have barn cats/dogs? Are they fixed? Are boarders allowed to bring their own dogs?

Health and Wellness Questions

These questions specifically outline the barn's policies and procedures regarding herd wellness. Equine parasites are transferred from horse to horse when they share the same pasture; therefore, most facilities require all boarders to be on the same type of deworming program. The same is true for vaccinations-- since many diseases can be transmitted very easily between horses sharing a facility, many barn owners require boarders to administer certain vaccines on a specific schedule to prevent a mass outbreak. Other facilities require horses who travel to shows or events to receive additional vaccines.

Additionally, many facilities require a brief quarantine for new horses, along with a negative Coggins test and a health certificate signed by a vet. A Coggins test checks for Equine Infectious Anemia, an extremely serious virus that is transmitted by flies. Some horses are carriers of this disease without ever presenting symptoms. There is no cure or treatment for EIA, and it can be fatal. A horse who receives a positive Coggins test will either need to be euthanized or quarantined for the rest of its life. Given the severity of the consequences, you'll need to make sure there's enough time for the Coggins to process before planning your horse's move.

These questions will ensure that you know exactly what is expected of you before your horse ever sets foot in the barn.

- What kind of deworming program do you follow?
- What vaccines do you require?
- What is your quarantine protocol for new horses?
- What type of protocol do you have for pest prevention and control, such as mice, cockroaches, flies, bots, and other regional concerns?
- Is there an extra charge for requesting a fly mask to be used on my horse?

Equipment Questions

Some barns provide certain types of equipment, while others provide none at all. It's a good idea to ask what is considered "community" property that is shared amongst boarders, and what you are expected to provide for yourself and your horse.

- Do I need to provide my own stall cleaning equipment (fork, bucket, cart, wheelbarrow, etc)?
- Where do I dispose of manure?
- Who is responsible for cleaning the arena/public areas?
- Will I need to bring my own water and feed buckets?
- If so, what type of buckets are preferred?
- Do you require hay nets?
- May I provide a salt or mineral block for my horse in his stall?

Community Questions

Besides the equine caretaking, you need to enjoy the human aspect of your new boarding facility as well. Nearly every barn has a set of rules that makes perfect sense, such as "no running in the barn," or "do not feed horses that are not your own," but some have rules that are very specific to the facility. These may not make sense at first, but there is always a very good reason behind every barn rule- just make sure you ask and understand!

- What are the barn rules?
- Do you have a dress code?
- What disciplines do the other boarders study?
- What is the guest policy?

Other Questions

Here are some questions that may not apply to every barn but can be great follow ups when discussing the ins and outs of daily life at a new facility. I wanted to include these just in case they apply to you, your horse, or the facility.

- Do you offer trailer parking or a trailer share program? What is the cost?
- Are there onsite shows/camps/clinics? Is participation mandatory?
- Do you offer travel to shows off-site?
- Do you organize group trail rides or other casual/social events?
- Do you have barn-shared equipment, such as brushes, fly spray, or leg wraps? If so, how often are they cleaned/replenished?
- Is there laundry on-site? If so, what are the laundry policies?
- What are some trusted local resources for supplies/feed/etc?
- Do you have any discount programs with equine product suppliers?
- Is there a tack room? Is it heated? Is it locked?

Some of these questions may be self-explanatory once you're onsite with the facility owner or barn manager, but others may not be as evident in plain view. I encourage anyone to ask as many questions as you can think of-- after all, you're basically finding a new apartment for your horse and all of their equipment. Take your time touring, and don't be afraid to call back to ask additional questions. You may have to look at a few different locations, but eventually, you will find the ideal place for your horse to call home!

I HAVE A
HORSE...
NOW WHAT?

How Grooming, Training, Riding,
and Equine Competitive Activities
Can Build a Lifelong Bond

MEREDITH HILL

CONTENTS

INTRODUCTION

I have had sole responsibility over many horses in my life. If you read the first book in this series, *Before Your Horse Comes Home: Introductory Horse Care for Beginners,* you've already been introduced to my first horse and our bittersweet short story together. But there have been other horses since then. Dolly went on to be a field hunter for a young girl. Maxwell, the ancient Appaloosa, became a family pet after the youngest son fell in love with him. There was Jacob, the naughty eventer who had plenty of brains but very few good ideas. Then, there was the accidental thoroughbred I bought from an internet ad while I was out of town. Today, I enjoy the company of Red, a rescued racehorse I bought for $10 and a hug, and Belle, a registered Quarter Horse who would like everyone to appreciate that she is a princess.

One of the top questions I'm asked about horses is, "What do you do with them all?" My answer surprises people: I enjoy them. People then respond with the following questions, "Do you take them to competitions? Do you have a lot of ribbons?" I have taken them to competitions, yes. I have a fair amount of ribbons. But in my case, it's not about competition; instead, it's about having fun.

I was raised in a very "non-horsey" home. That is to say, my parents weren't exactly keen about my enthusiasm for large, stinky beasts who could potentially end my life if I took a wrong step. In a way, I don't blame them— with a bleak outlook like that, there's hardly any room for understanding the abundant joy and comfort that I get from horses. Therefore, I was always trying to find a way to get a "horse fix". There was much wheedling and cajoling through my younger years, and once I had the opportunity, I started doing barn chores in exchange for riding time. Many professional equestrians got their start this way, so I figured it was a matter of time before my dedication and determination led me towards superstardom.

But then something happened that changed the course of my history: I attended my first horse show as a rider. I had been to loads of horse shows before, in the capacity of a groom/assistant/runner/barn hand, and I had the time of my life. There was always something going on. I spent the day dashing from ring to ring to make sure riders had all the supplies they needed, keeping horses and humans fed and hydrated, and keeping all of our equipment accounted for and hopefully in the right place.

Riding in a show was different. After you warm up, it's a lot of standing around waiting for your class or round to be called. The weather is invariably too hot or too cold for what you're wearing, so you spend the day shivering in clothing that's only practical for the show ring, or drenched in sweat, gasping for air. The restroom is always at the furthest point from the ring in which your classes are being called, and the chaos that is so charming from the ground– a cacophony of eager and anxious people, horses, and dogs with very different agendas– becomes a safety hazard.

Despite the fact that I placed well in my classes, I didn't find horse shows fun. Hunter/ jumper riding had more or less been foisted upon me through collaboration between my father and my riding instructor when I was just seven years old. My father thought the outfits were nice and boring– black jackets and beige breeches with tall black leather boots– and my instructor thought I had the right level of precision and perfectionism to make it around the ring with finesse. While I thought I had been having a good time, maybe I was simply in the wrong sport.

So I hopped in every saddle that was offered to me for several years. I learned a thing or two about reining. I hung out with some competitive trail riders. I took lessons with a show jumper and learned about tight spaces and fast paces. Western pleasure. Gaited horses. Then, one day I found myself in a very dark barn– lit by just two arena floodlights– with a very large 18-hand gray horse, having my very first dressage lesson. It all clicked- This was what I wanted to do with my life.

Dressage has been compared to dancing with a horse, and from the ground, it looks like the horse and rider are performing lovely, floating steps. In the saddle, however, it's a matter of relaxing your body and brain while simultaneously using every named part of your body and flowing both with and against the motion of the horse to create shapes, paces, and movements. Dancing is a fair assessment, but I'd be more inclined to call it yoga.

At the same time, I'm still not moved by the spirit of competition. I rode in dressage shows throughout my intercollegiate career and continued competing in hunter/jumper shows as well. But, I was bored. My ribbons resided at my parents' houses. I skipped the regional shows I qualified for because I didn't want to go. My college coach– who is still my mentor to this day– didn't push me to go because she understood. Sometimes it's not about the shows.

Instead, I wanted to have fun. I wanted to have the most fun possible, in the safest possible way, with horses I truly understood. And that right there is enough work to keep me busy every day.

There's nothing wrong with showing. Many of my horsey friends thrive on regular trips into the show pen. It is thrilling to hear your name called over the loudspeaker,watch your points accumulate, get end-of-the-year awards and prizes, and have measurable improvement in your riding and career.

There's also nothing wrong with not showing, or showing rarely. There's nothing wrong with barrel racing in an English saddle if you feel like it, or riding with no saddle at all. In fact, you can own a horse for its entire life and never ride it once, and that's perfectly fine. While there's a lot of pressure in the horse world to be the best in the world, I don't agree with that philosophy.

I believe, as do many equestrians, that the top consideration of horse ownership should be the partnership you build. I've noticed a sad decline in the number of people who truly bond with and understand their horses. When I started giving lessons years ago, I would ask riders who had owned or been working with their horses for months or years what their horses liked. What was their personality? What did they enjoy? They couldn't tell me. "He likes food, I guess?" "He likes it when I take him outside to eat grass." "She likes winning ribbons."

While I don't like coming off as preachy, I do feel it's very important to know your horse in a real way. My first horse hated peppermints. Maxwell hated hugs. Dolly liked it when I gave her scratches right above her tail. Red has two specific two very specific favorite brushes. Belle thinks zippers are the best invention ever. Just like any living being, horses have preferences and patterns in their lives. When you share your life with one of these animals, it's your responsibility to learn what makes them happy.

At the same time, you don't have to stand there and stare at your horse to receive that information. Interacting with your horses in a meaningful way will tell you much more about their personality than watching what the critter does of his own volition. Therefore, I encourage every horse owner to work with their horses. You ask, "Now what?" I say, "Work with your horse."

In this book, we'll look at all of the different meanings of that phrase. "Work" doesn't mean you have to plow the fields, jump a 5-foot fence, or start schooling canter pirouettes... but you can if you want to. It is my goal to empower horse people of every level of experience and understanding to learn how to spend meaningful time with their horses.

We'll start with the basis for it all: groundwork. Being able to control and understand your horse while you both have your feet on the ground is the foundation from which everything you do behind the reins is built. Furthermore, groundwork establishes boundaries, safety, and confidence.

Then, we'll take a look at a variety of different equine sports. Whether you choose to dip your toes in the basics or head full steam into a competitive lifestyle is up to you and your horses. We'll look at what the sport entails, the type of training and movement required, the equipment needed, and what type of professional can help you get to the level where you and your horse feel most comfortable. It's a lot to cover, so consider this an introduction to your new favorite sport rather than a comprehensive guide to doing absolutely anything with a horse.

Lastly, I'll provide you with a few insights into getting into the horse community. As always, there will be a "Resources" section to help you network, research, and learn more about equine events in your area, or in general. As I mentioned in my first book, learning should be a constant for those who aspire to have long, happy, and healthy relationships with their horses.

You have a horse... now what? Now you start having the most amazing time of your life with your new big, stinky, and fuzzy buddy.

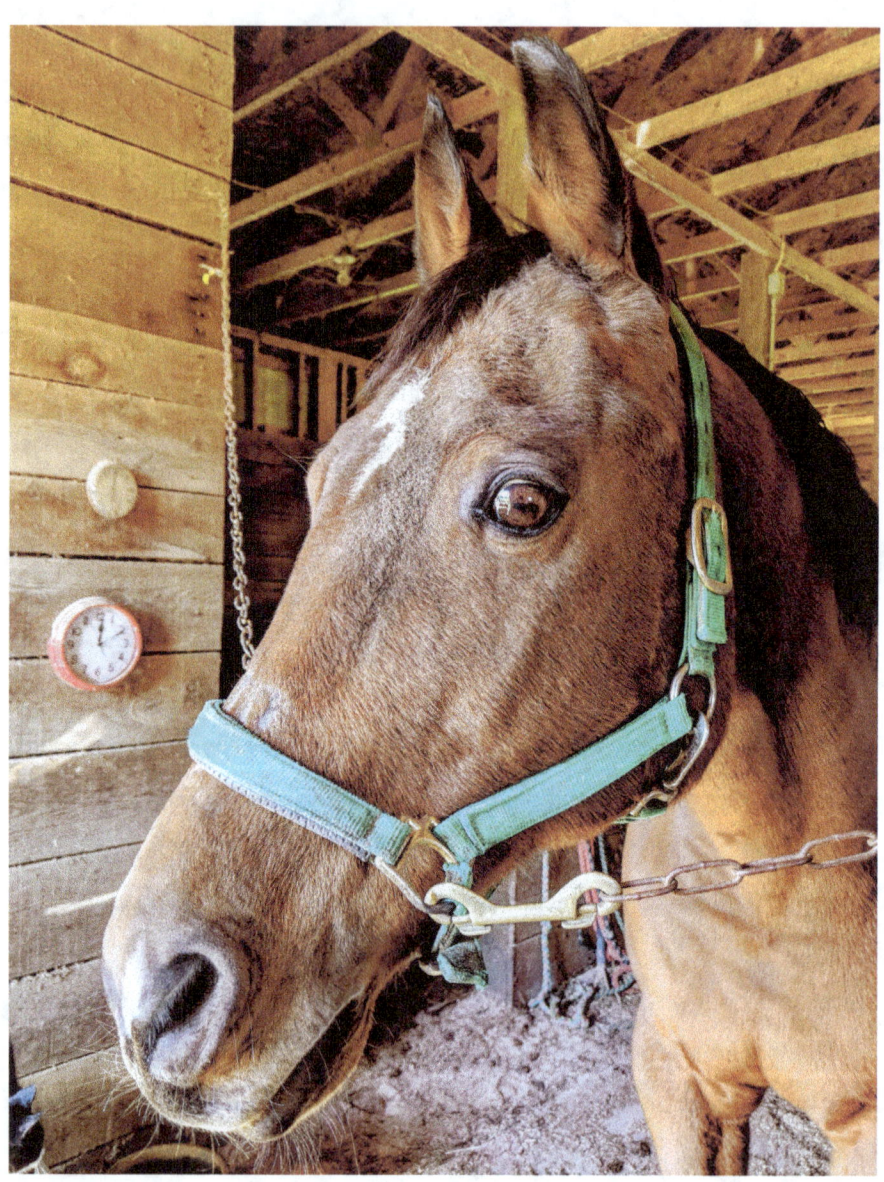

PART 1: GETTING TO KNOW YOUR HORSE

How do you "get to know" a horse? Do you walk into its stall and say, "Hi, horsey. My name is (your name). I'm going to call you (horse's name). How do you do?"

You might laugh, but it's not a half bad idea.

Early in my equine career, I had an instructor who forbade us from talking to the horses. "They don't understand what you're saying, and you're not allowed to use voice cues when you show, anyway." Fair points, but since this particular trainer, I've not met a single person who *doesn't* talk to their horse.

Maybe your horse doesn't understand your full introduction, but horses, like any animal, can learn to recognize a variety of cues, whether spoken or unspoken. Horses, in particular, are keen on picking up specific motions, words, and the tone of your voice. Belle, for example, has been trained to respond to a variety of clicks, smoochy noises, and hums to perform various gaits. Racehorses are trained to urinate when you whistle. While a horse may not have an appreciative understanding of *Hamlet's* "To be or not to be" soliloquy, he can be trained to recognize a variety of words and sounds.

Furthermore, something interesting happens when we speak out loud around our horse: we act like ourselves. Our observant horses pick up on our tones and our moods and respond. I have seen many professionals use harsh tones of voice to get a horse to knock off naughty behavior, while I have seen a soothing voice help calm a nervous horse. Often, the way we speak and act align closely, and your horse will respond to tension, anger, sadness, nervousness, and calmness accordingly.

Therefore, my first recommendation is to talk to your horse. Tell it what you want it to do. Share with it how you're feeling. Explain what you're going to do during your time together in a particular session. Ask why it has a particular bad habit, or keeps doing something annoying. That early instructor was right in that they aren't going to participate in conversational English dialogue, but they will respond. They'll respond to key words they know, and they'll learn about your moods and actions.

However, don't make the conversation one-sided. Listen to your horse, too. Horses have a lot to say. Whether it's throwing their head as high in the air as they can to signal discomfort, or sticking out their bottom lip when you find a good scratchy spot, horses are constantly communicating. Think about how they talk to each other too. Horses mainly speak to each other with body language. They bump into, nibble on, kick at, rear at, dart away from, and lick each other to share their preferences with their herdmates. And just as you communicate with them in the language you know, they'll "talk" to you in their language as well.

So, getting to know your horse is a matter of learning how to talk to each other, even though you don't speak the same language. That doesn't mean you should stop speaking your own language— you just need to spend some quality time together so you can each learn what each other's sound or gesture means.

And that, in a nutshell, is the foundation for every great human-equine relationship.

Let's get started on learning the basics of communication between horse and human.

SECTION 1: SALUTATIONS AND GREETINGS

Have you ever watched two horses meet each other for the first time? It can be pretty dramatic, depending on the characters involved.

Typically, it starts with sniffing. Nostrils flared to process as much of each other's scent as possible, they breathe loudly, assessing each other with arched necks. If a threat is imminent, that arched neck position will allow them to retreat quickly, or lash out with teeth bared, depending on whether flight or fight is more appropriate.

There will be some snapping, grunting, squealing, and a noise I can only describe as "honking". They may strike at each other with their front hooves, or turn their hindquarters and kick into the other's face. As a human standing on the ground, it can be more than a little disconcerting. Horses can be brutal to each other in their introductions, but that's part of establishing their roles in the herd.

Some horsemanship experts feel that your horse should see you as the "head of the herd." You should be the alpha, and your horse should submit to you. I don't entirely like the way that sounds, though I think I know what these experts are trying to impart. Your horse should understand not to snap at you, strike at you with his hooves, or act like a general fool when you appear. However, there's no reason for your presence to be intimidating to your horse.

In this section, I'll share some tips for meeting your horse on common ground. I don't claim to be a horsemanship expert, but as someone who has worked with horses around the country for over thirty years, I admit I have a fair amount of experience with the topic of creating a decent working relationship with horses I have never met before. I'm not going to solve all of your problems, but I intend to give you some hope and understanding.

I also encourage you to work with a professional, especially if this is your very first horse, or you're new to horses in general. Working with a rank horse can be very dangerous, and I recommend having a buddy around in case of an emergency. If your horse is asking you questions you cannot answer, it is appropriate and strongly encouraged to enlist the help of someone with more experience on the matter.

I recommend starting slowly when meeting your new horse for the first time, so let's take it step-by-step from saying "hello" to learning how to speak the same language fluently.

Chapter 1: An Introduction to Introductions

First impressions are everything. When you meet someone for the first time, the way each of you behave and interact will become a lasting memory.

This is actually true regardless of the species involved in the interaction. We've all seen dogs sniff each other's derriére, or cats spit and wave at each other. When a horse meets a new horse, they sniff each other's faces, paw at the ground, squeal, and even nip a little to help them understand their relationship to one another. Sometimes equine relationship building involves more physical interaction with running, fighting, and kicking used as measures to demonstrate dominance and tolerance.

Obviously, as smaller, far more fragile beings, we want to avoid getting in a kick-fight with a larger, incredibly powerful horse. Therefore, the way you approach your new horse really matters, especially as you're starting to get to know each other.

For the first few months of your new partnership, I recommend exercising caution around your horse. Be on high alert because your horse will likely be as well. As a prey animal in a new place, he likely has no idea what's really going on. He woke up, ate breakfast, walked into a box, the box started moving, and now he's here. Unless your new horse is an experienced show horse who has been dragged all over creation and is used to waking up in new barns, this is going to take some getting used to.

My first recommendation is to let the horse smell you. Every time you approach him, let him sniff your outstretched hands. Some horses will try to get into your face as they would with another horse, but as a human, you have the right to decide if you will permit this behavior or not. Some people strictly enforce a barrier around their person that the horse cannot enter. Similarly, some horses have no interest in entering your personal space anyway.

Others, myself included, allow horses to touch them once they've established a few basic rules, namely: no teeth. Horses communicate a lot with their teeth since they can't use their hands or fingers to gesture like humans do. Different nips mean different things and can actually be a sign of affection in some cases. Unfortunately, humans have very thin skin compared to horses and even the most loving bites hurt us. Therefore, do not encourage a horse to nip at you. Should your horse start to explore your coat, hat, or glasses with his mouth, a gentle flat hand pop to the nose and a "NO BITE" command should do the trick. If it doesn't, you might have a biter on your hands. That means no hand feeding treats and dodging that mouth until it learns to stay shut. In extreme cases, you may wish to work with a professional behavioralist to help your horse unlearn this vice.

So, here you are in front of your new horse, who has sniffed you completely. Now what? This is where you interact with your equine companion. Talk to him. Stroke his neck and face and move around his body, but be sure to keep an eye on the horse's body language as you do so. Ears upright and swiveling mean he's paying attention and listening– that's a good sign. Ears turned backwards and slightly horizontal mean he's not entirely happy with what you're doing, but willing to entertain your thoughts unless they escalate. Ears plastered to the head completely are a sign to stay away.

Just as some humans have a strictly enforced personal space, so do many horses, at least until they get to know you. If you've only worked with lesson horses or horses that deal with a lot of people on a regular basis, they'll probably have more relaxed rules about who can touch them and where. This part might be over quickly as they learn to recognize you as a "regular human," who will interact with them on a daily basis. Horses might be one of the more reactive creatures on this planet, but they're definitely not without intelligence!

Therefore, don't be surprised at how much or how little time it takes for your horse to accept you into his personal space. Don't be shocked if he spooks when you drop a brush, or if he turns his hindquarters to you and becomes offended when you walk into his stall to clean it. Horses love routine, so it may take your new buddy some time to learn the ins and outs of his new home.

You can make this easier for him by greeting him each time you go out to the barn. I actually holler, "Good morning, Ponies!" to the herd I care for each time I come out to feed. Some of them even greet me in return. As I mentioned earlier, I'm a strong believer in talking to horses. Not only does it set the mood, but it helps you maintain clarity and focus when working with your horse. Best case scenario? Your horse learns the sound of your voice and your body language.

Worst case scenario? Your horse tunes you out and daydreams about carrots and green pasture as far as the eye can see. As far as I can tell, it's not really much of a loss!

Chapter 2 : Reach out and Touch Your Horse

Another great way to bond with your new horse is through the act of grooming. There are so many schools of thought on the necessity of and proper technique for grooming that I can hardly cover it all here. However, since this can be a fantastic way for you and your horse to get to know each other, I'm going to include the basics.

Personally, I see grooming as a great opportunity to check up on your horse. As you brush them from head to hoof, you can check them over for any interesting heat, swelling, or abrasions. Horses can be shockingly clumsy, even within the confines of a stall. In fact, you might notice that a horse who rarely leaves his stall has swollen legs. Known commonly as "stocking up," this swelling is a harmless accumulation of blood and other fluids. In most cases, letting your horse walk around will help the swelling go down.

But, regular grooming of your horse will help you learn the differences between something simple, such as stocking up, versus a real problem. Swelling and heat can be signs of all sorts of trouble, from an abscess in the hoof to a puncture wound or tendon injury. Knowing your horse's topography can help you know when to call the vet and when to cold hose and hand walk your companion.

Additionally, brushing your horse can help keep his coat healthy, although some experts disagree on how frequently or with how much vigor you should brush your horse. Here are my basic thoughts on grooming:

- A daily once-over– including a basic dust off and hoof pick– is good for catching problems or injuries before they become a big deal. If you're going to be working with your horse, make sure there isn't any dirt, burrs, or other debris in the areas where you and the tack will come in contact with the horse's body. Just as you wouldn't want to run laps with a pinecone in your pants, your horse prefers not to chafe while he works too.

- If your horse is covered in mud or dirt, clean it off. While it's true that wild horses run around muddy with no problem, your domesticated horse needs to be able to fluff his coat when it's cold, sweat when it's hot, and slick the water off of his skin when it's raining.

- A regular, thorough brushing can help keep skin healthy. "Regular" can mean many things, though. Red has a history of skin fungus, so he gets a thorough grooming far more often than Belle, who has never had problems.

- If you live in a climate where your horse grows and sheds a thick, shaggy winter coat, help relieve him of that extra fluff when temperatures warm up. Yes, he'll shed naturally, but if you're planning on increasing his workload, remember that he's wearing his winter coat while he works. He'll sweat more and become tired more easily, just as you would if you wore a snow suit in warmer temperatures. Clipping a horse's sweatiest areas can be very helpful for preventing overheating or getting a chill from being too wet.

- Shampooing and conditioning a horse's mane, tail, or body isn't something you need to do frequently unless you are going to be hitting the shows, or your horse has skin/hair issues that you're addressing. Horses produce oils naturally that help keep their skin and hair healthy, so while it might be helpful to fully wash an exceptionally muddy or sweaty horse, you don't need to worry about throwing your horse in the bathtub every night. In fact, please don't– it would probably break the porcelain.

Do I really groom my horse every single day? Most of the time, no. When the weather is warm and their coats are short, it's much easier to check them for flesh wounds. Plus, both of my horses are actively working in my trainer's lesson program, which means my trainer and keen students are also grooming and interacting with them daily.

One of the most important things about the act of grooming is that it can be some of the best bonding time between a horse and a human. You're both relaxed and sharing space together. You can take this time to understand what kind of touching your horse enjoys, and which he despises. Red, for example, loves this thin rubber nubby grooming glove I have and hates regular curry combs. If you rubbed his face with It all day, it might not be long enough for him. Belle, on the other hand, likes really stiff body brushes and will lean her shoulders into a nice hard brushstroke. They're all different, and the only way to really find these connections is through jumping in and trying various brushes and techniques.

I encourage any first time horse owner to get a variety of brushes, including a curry comb, stiff body brush,soft face brush, and hoof pick with a brush on the end of it. Personally, I like to pick out my brushes in person, so I can see how each tool feels in my hands. For example, bigger brushes can be harder to grip for people with smaller hands. You don't need to buy the super-expensive brushes at first, unless you really want to and your budget permits. Look for something that will stand up to heavy fur and mud removal, but expect that at some point, it will be dropped in manure, stepped on, and eventually lost in the darkest corners of your tack trunk or brush bins.

Over time, you'll discover that you've accumulated an uncanny number of your horse's favorite brushes, which will all look ratty and gross compared to the ver-sions your horse doesn't like as much. As you take stock of your brushes, you'll likely call up certain memories associated with each one. Like the time you dropped that blue brush under your horse, and you weren't sure how best to retrieve it. Or the time your horse came in super muddy, and you were so glad you had that one green scrubby thing.

These memories will serve as your proof that the time spent fussing over your horse's hair and hooves hasn't been time spent in vain. You've learned a lot about your horse in that time. You should be familiar with your horse's body and the way he acts when you brush here or scritchy-scratch there. Or how his lower lip sticks out when you brush right there, and he stubbornly refuses to pick up that hoof on the first try. That's getting to know your horse. That's building a relationship. And it's all right there, at the end of the brush.

Chapter 3 : Building Friendship through Groundwork

The word "groundwork" is flung around in the equestrian community like an old rag. Everyone who has been around horses for more than a few years has their own version of groundwork that they will swear is the one and only way to work with a horse. While that's definitely not true, these so-called experts aren't exactly wrong, either.

You see, groundwork is really just communication exercises between humans and horses. As you look around and think of all the humans you interact with on a daily basis, you'll realize that everyone has a different communication style. For example, some might speak too loudly, and others might speak too softly. Some people might have a tone that comes across as sharp and bossy, while others seem dismissive and uninterested in the conversation. Some people speak very quickly, while others speak very slowly.

In fact, you might find that you have to work harder to understand some of your acquaintances than others. You might have to ask the fast talkers or low talkers to repeat themselves. You might get impatient and angry when the slow talkers take their time getting to the point. While horses don't speak a human language, they have a fine-tuned ability to learn body language, tone of voice, and some verbal commands. However, just as you might have no idea what your human friend says when they mumble, your horse might not have any clue what you're trying to impart upon him at first. You need to learn how to communicate with each other, hence the groundwork.

My personal thought is that each horse needs to know at least a few basic ground manners. I need to be sure that whatever horse I'm leading from his stall to the pasture is going to walk politely next to me. When I need him to stop, he will stop. When I remove the lead rope from his halter, I need him to wait politely for me to step away before he takes off. If I drop the lead rope for any reason, I need him to stand still and wait for me to pick the rope back up.

However, groundwork can go far beyond that. I've taught Red how to shake hands, and he'll follow me around an obstacle course without a halter or lead rope. Belle can spin, side step, back up, and follow me based on my body position. Both of my horses free lunge without a rope, and they switch between gaits based on voice commands and hand gestures. People do all sorts of "tricks" with their horses, but at the end of the day, they're establishing and fine-tuning their communication with each other.

There are many experts out there who would be thrilled for you to invest your time and money into their training programs. If you choose to go this route, I highly recommend that you take the time to investigate the trainer. Don't just watch a few videos, but Google the trainer's name to see what kind of reputation they have as a human. Put yourself in your horse's steel bar shoes– consider how you would feel applying the trainer's techniques on yourself. Horses aren't at the same cognitive position as humans, but if what the trainer is doing offends you, then chances are it will also annoy your horse.

Most groundwork experts can, however, agree on some of the basics. For example, if you are leading your horse with a rope attached to his halter, he should be cheerfully moving at a similar pace with his head aligned with your right shoulder. When you stop, he should stop. When you start walking again and ask him to move forward, he should do so. So, what do you do if your horse doesn't have these magical command buttons?

In many instances, your horse will follow you out of curiosity or anticipation of where you might be going. If your horse has a specific routine such as going out to their field after breakfast, they'll probably be inclined to follow along very politely because they know where they're going and why. But as a human who is much smaller and slower than a horse, you want them to follow along politely even if they have no idea where they're going. If you discover that your horse doesn't want to leave the barn through a specific door or leading your horse becomes a battle of wills, you might want to revisit basic groundwork.

Start small. As in, start in a small area where if your horse gets loose, it's not going to be a big problem. An arena, round pen, or smaller paddock is ideal for groundwork because you can allow your horse to make choices about his movement without risking him deciding he's done and running off into the sunset.

I recommend taking every safety precaution you can as well. Wear thick leather gloves if you're going to be doing work with a lead rope or lunge line. Choose ropes that are comfortable in your hands, and not too light and thin or too heavy and bulky. A helmet can protect your head in case things get weird. Establish an escape route. Wear appropriate footwear– absolutely no sandals.

Also, be prepared to let go. Our number one reaction when working with a bolting horse is to hang on. This is bad because in most cases, horses have no problem dragging your body weight behind them as their adrenaline-filled brains urge them to gallop far away from what frightens them. While letting go might not be ideal when a small pen or arena is not available, it is much safer than your terrified, frantic horse dragging you on your face at top speed.

Start slow as well. Take just a few steps at a time. When reinforcing a horse's ability to lead politely, attach the lead rope to his halter. Walk forward a few steps and ask him to walk alongside you. Then stop. When you stop, your horse should stop. Walk five steps, then stop again. Stand still. Make your horse wait for you to urge him to move forward again. Walk ten steps and repeat the exercise. Vary the number of steps you take at a time and how long you wait before walking off again.

If your horse has been trained well, a quick refresher with his new human should be enough to remind him what good manners are and the difference between "stop", "wait", and "go". If your horse is particularly excited by his new surroundings, you might need to repeat yourself a few times. And if your horse has never been taught good manners, you'll be starting from scratch.

If he's tossing his head around, jogging in place, trying to go up, down, or sideways, or trying to dash off, you might want to put a chain over his nose. The point of the chain isn't to hurt the horse, but rather, to create pressure he can't ignore. Remember– you're small and a different species. You need to be able to command your horse in a way he will recognize. Since horses use teeth, hooves, and loud noises to get each other's attention, you need to step up your game from muttering curse words and pulling, since these are very ignorable when you're 1,200 pounds and desperately interested in what your buddy is doing in that field over there. You should be able to give the chain a quick tug from the ground to get your horse's attention. If you leave a mark, you're using far too much pressure.

Likewise, if your horse balks and refuses to move forward, you might want to bring a long lunge whip along to encourage the back end of your horse to go forward without putting yourself directly behind the horse. Again, you're not trying to cause the horse pain, but create a sense of pressure that he'll want to move away from.

Remember that at the very core of their being, horses are prey animals. Their first instinct is to remove themselves from the vicinity of intimidating things. The end of the whip, though logically not frightening, mimics scary things in nature just closely enough that your horse is hard-wired to respect it, even if he doesn't yet respect you. The whip is also much longer than our human arm span, which means you don't have to be close to the horse's danger zones when you use this tool.

The goal of any tools you use when schooling groundwork is not to be mean or violent, but to be safe. You want your horse's attention on you so that he doesn't accidentally run you over, step on you, or bolt off taking your arm and shoulder with him. Leading horses with bad ground manners is a very prominent cause for human injury, especially those to the hand, wrist, or shoulder. Nearly every equestrian over a certain age has lost full range of motion of their neck and shoulders, and as someone who fits in that category, I encourage you to avoid injury. No horse is 100% predictable, but a horse with good manners is more likely to react to scary situations more appropriately.

Over time, your horse may be willing to follow you without a lead rope, stopping, walking, jogging, and doing patterns based only on your cues. Bear in mind, however, this won't happen immediately. Many new equestrians become very frustrated when they start working with an unfamiliar horse because it can take months or even years to develop a truly harmonious bond with a horse. Continue to put in the work, repeat the exercises, and be patient— you are learning to speak a language that neither of you have spoken before.

In fact, the "Stop/Go" exercise I've just outlined is an exercise you'll want to repeat frequently, until you and your horse are on the same page. Every time I work with any horse, I do a quick check on where their brains are by walking a few steps, stopping, waiting, and walking off again to see how quickly and completely they respond to my cues. Even though I'm on the ground next to them, their reaction to these simple commands lets me know what has their attention and whether they're feeling peppy, sluggish, or are completely focused on me.

This is, of course, just one of the many types of groundwork exercises you can practice with your horse, but one that I feel is at the foundation of every relationship between a human and a horse, no matter how short or temporary. As someone who has worked with many horses in many situations, I cannot stress enough the importance of feeling confident when leading a horse, even if it's just a few steps. The more you practice groundwork, the more capable you'll feel, regardless of whether you're working with your trusty steed of dozens of years, or a new beast who has just come off the trailer. And as for the horse, he'll be pleased to know who's in charge around here and to whom he should address his attention.

Chapter 4 : What If My Horse Doesn't Like Me?

It's actually somewhat concerning how often I hear people complain that their horse "doesn't like them." Or, if I'm speaking with someone who has limited contact with horses, they might whine, "Horses just don't like me."

Some horses don't like people. Some horses don't like certain people. But if your own personal horse doesn't like you, you really shouldn't gloss over that fact. And if all horses universally dislike you, perhaps you should address the common denominator.

Nearly every undesirable equine behavior traces back to the fact that they are prey animals. They are naturally highly reactive to things that trouble them. A lot of things trouble them. You should not be one of those things.

When people tell me their horse doesn't like them, I ask them if they like their horse. It's a harsh question, but a very serious one as well. If you don't bond with your horse through simple activities such as grooming and groundwork, it is far more likely that you two will not develop a great relationship. Sometimes, that is not anyone's fault. I have known several horses that simply wanted nothing to do with me— either because they were bonded to another person, or because they had been in an environment that led them to not trust any human. However, in most cases, spending a significant amount of time with your horse will at the very least help you establish a working relationship.

The concept of "joining up" has changed faces several times within my three decades of working with horses. When I was a young equestrian, I was encouraged to spend time with my horses outside of working with them. I'd see other riders eating a sandwich outside their horse's stall, standing outside their horse's stall and idly stroking his face while chatting with barn friends, and sitting on a stool reading a horse magazine to figure out their next training ride— essentially, we were encouraged to just hang out with our horses.

Then came the "Horse Whisperers" of the 1990s, and suddenly there were several different theories of what "joining up" meant and how to achieve it. Some believe it means making your horse move his feet and body towards his human, while others insist your horse should move away from pressure. Some equine behaviorists think the horse should see you as herd leader, while others feel horses gain confidence by exploring on their own.

So, who's right? In my experience of attending dozens of clinics and working with many different experts, everyone has valid points. I personally train my horses to move towards me **and** away from me, based on different cues. I want my horses to follow me around, but I don't want them so dependent on me that they are incapable of thinking when I'm not there to tell them what to do.

My own personal "joining up" exercise combines a lot of these ideas. I do hang out with my horses each day. I talk to them and interact with them, or stand by their stall and give them scritchy scratches on their ears while I talk to my trainer. I see no reason not to do this. But when I work with them, I occasionally take them off the lead in the arena to see what happens.

Bear in mind, I only do this with horses who have manners, and who I trust will not immediately run me over when we're sharing a space. I'd recommend being solid on "Stop/Go" commands before sharing a small area with any horse at liberty.

You might be wondering what to expect to happen, and honestly, it depends on how your horse is feeling that day. Red is especially trustworthy at liberty, and some days, he'll wander around the arena and sniff things while I do chores. Sometimes he'll roll in the dirt, bounce back to his feet and gallop around until his inner "yeehaw" has been expressed. Other times, he follows me around, casually observing my weird two-legged behaviors. When I'm done, I give him the command to come back (if he's not already lurking behind me or waiting patiently at the gate for me), and we head back to his stall.

What do we get out of this? Today, it mainly reaffirms our trust for each other. I am confident that he's not going to do anything harmful or inappropriate, and he knows his boundaries and when to listen to me.

When we were first introduced, he would spend a lot of his time hanging out in the corner of the arena, ignoring me. I'd walk over to greet him, and he'd swivel his ears. Sometimes he'd let me approach, and other times he told me to back off. Other times, he would abruptly pivot and gallop off in the other direction.

The point of the exercise isn't necessarily to always catch the horse or have the horse come on command. Instead, it's about learning to communicate. Let's look at it as if both parties were human, but spoke different languages. Say, for example, you speak Dutch, but your coworker speaks Spanish. It would be as if your goal is to learn how to communicate with each other in fluent Korean. Think about how you would go about such a task. There would be a lot of gesturing and communicating through body language. You'd make a lot of mistakes and so would your coworker. You would both get frustrated with the task. And most of all, you would expect it to take some time.

Before you start asking a horse to respond to your complex commands in a work environment, you should understand how to communicate in the first place. Sometimes behavior that is described as "naughty" is just a misunderstanding. In the dressage world, for example, upper level horses are cued for a canter with the inside leg, while lower level horses or horses that do not exclusively compete in dressage use a cue from the leg by the wall. Riders who are accustomed to horses trained to spur stop will be in for a surprise when they get more forward action from a horse who is trained the other way around. Without knowing a horse's particular language, you could be confusing the horse for a very long time before you realize you're simply asking the question in a language he doesn't understand.

The concept of "joining up," in all of its various formats and definitions, nearly always boils down to getting to a point where you and your horse understand each other. Once you have the ability to understand each other, you have unlocked the potential to build a relationship.

Does this mean your horse is going to love you, fawn over you, and neigh joyfully every time you enter the barn? No. There may still be days when you flat out don't like each other. But, there are probably days when you don't like your boss, brother, or next-door neighbor too.

We all have moods, opinions, ideas, and preferences. Some people feel you should train your horse so that he is unable to express any of those. I've met horses like that and understand the means used to create that behavior, but I personally do not advocate it. Instead— however New Age or suspicious this might seem— I think it's much more meaningful to learn how to communicate with your horse so that he is able to collaborate with you when you work together. In my opinion, a horse that reacts to danger is far safer than one who stands there and lets a disaster happen.

If you are under the impression that your horse doesn't like you, consider calling a truce and starting from the beginning. Get to know each other. Start back at the very beginning with regular grooming. Hang out together. Figure out what your horse likes, from treats to brushes to movements and more. Take the time to learn the language the two of you will be speaking for the rest of your lives together, and you might just find that your compatibility increases dramatically.

Author's Anecdote- Thawing the Ice Princess

The more I reflect, the more I realize there are several horses and ponies in my past who could be referred to as an "ice princess." Mares, in particular, are very hot-cold creatures. That is, they approve of what you're doing, or they despise you for existing. That's only slightly a hyperbole– I have known several riders and trainers who have refused to take on mares because of their perceived attitude.

I don't like to generalize, but I've found that when I'm experiencing a personality clash with a horse, that horse is female. Still, I have known several mares that I have loved deeply, including my very own Belle, who perhaps reigns supreme over all "ice princesses." Not only was she cold when I acquired her– she was completely frozen.

I met Belle many years ago when she was fresh from her first 60 days of training. My friend bought her as green broke, mainly for her bloodline. If Belle didn't excel in any equine sport, my friend was confident that she would at least be a good investment as a broodmare.

The trainer came, and I started noticing that she spent very little time working with Belle. Soon, it came to light that the trainer was afraid of riding Belle because when she made the horse mad, she would spook. Belle is pretty smart, so she just started acting like a fool when the trainer tried to work with her which scared her off. Since the trainer needed money, she lied to the owner about what she was doing and hadn't trained her a bit.

Belle's owner fired the trainer and took her to a small, quiet barn, where she calmly, slowly, and quietly worked with her one-on-one until the mare got her brain back. They competed at several shows and did very well. This is where I bow out of the story temporarily, as I began working with a new trainer and a new herd of horses. In fact, I more or less forgot about her until one day she showed up at my trainer's barn as a new lesson horse.

She was skinny and limping and plastered herself against the back wall of her stall for a few days. She was terrified of every creak and groan in the barn and snapped at people who entered her stall. Clearly, something had gone awry in the past several years. Even more obvious was the fact that Belle wasn't going to be used as a lesson horse any time soon.

Since I had worked with rescue horses, I was nominated to see if we could get Belle to come out of her shell. Motivated by my rage at whoever had gotten her to this state, I agreed.

The Stop/Go exercise was absolutely perfect. She was trained for horsemanship (which we'll explore in a bit), so she knew how to stop, wait, walk, ground tie, and do 180- and 360-degree turns on her hindquarters. But if I attempted to touch her, she would stop abruptly. Her body would freeze in place, except for her lower left eyelid which would tremble violently. That was her sign that things were not okay.

So I started letting her go in the arena to see what she would do. I realize this is in direct conflict with what I recommended earlier, and for a brief moment, I honestly wondered what I would do if she refused to be collected once we had reached a good stopping point.

Mercifully, that wasn't the case. The first day we did this, she ran to the gate connecting the main row of stalls to the arena in our barn. I tried to approach her, and she took off in a hurry to the other side of the arena. So I took a seat on one of the stools used for mounting blocks, and let her explore the arena.

First came the chaos. She didn't understand why she was loose, but she didn't have any good ideas as to what she should be doing at the moment, and the only other living creature around was just sitting there. She sped around the arena in fear of the unknown.

Then she decided to check out her environment. She sniffed jump standards along the wall, poles on the ground, and manure left behind by an ill-mannered student (it is polite to pick up manure in shared areas when you're done with them!). Every few strides, she'd look over to me to see what was going on, and if I had any input. I didn't.

Eventually, I stood up. This caused a new wave of chaos and investigation. I moved, and that wasn't quite as concerning. I moved more and more, and it became less and less worrisome to Belle. After about twenty minutes, she decided she really didn't care if I belted out "YMCA" by the Village People complete with choreography. I was no longer considered a threat, but I wasn't quite trustworthy yet.

Meanwhile, in the barn, I started hanging out by her stall door after feeding her. Not in a looming, malicious way— I wanted her to know that I was going to be present, but not necessarily interacting. I sat on a tack trunk and sent work emails, or called someone and chatted so she could get a feel for casual speech. It wasn't really extra effort because I was doing what I would usually do, but I made it a point for her to notice me doing it. I did it not because I believed we could magically meld our souls together, but because I wanted her to know my baseline. If all a horse hears is someone screaming at them, they're going to assume that screaming is how humans communicate. They'll either become aggressive and "scream" back, or avoid all contact and freeze. I wanted Belle to get out of the habit of thinking that everyone was screaming at her, and that we could just "talk" politely.

According to my notes, it took about a year for her to stop with the eye twitching. I've heard many horse people say that it's harder to undo someone else's horrible training than to do it right the first time, and I agree. Belle is much more personable than she was when she first arrived, but there are still days when she tries to respond to pressure with her teeth. She's a polite and beloved lesson horse, but there are times she becomes overwhelmed with information and reacts with a small spook. We'll continue to work on these things for the rest of our days together, I'm sure.

I've worked with horses that spook, bolt, rear, buck, dance sideways, slam riders into the wall, and more. But the most terrifying reaction is none at all. You don't know what to prepare for because the next step after freezing is usually the equine equivalent of a psychotic break, all adrenaline and brain stem with no cognitive function.

Every time Belle gives me a little snuggle with her muzzle, or pops her head out of her stall window to say hi when she hears my car pull up, it reminds me that while not every horse and human bond is the same, it still has the chance to be a positive and inviting situation for both creatures.

SECTION 2 : DECIDING WHAT TO DO WITH YOUR HORSE

So, what are your plans for your horse?

For some people, the answer to this question is straightforward and immediate. "I plan to work up through the Pony Club levels." "I would like to be ready to ride a First Level dressage test by April." "I'm going to wait for her to finish growing, then send her to my trainer to get her started with reining."

Others of us really don't have long-term goals. I ended up buying Belle as a complete fluke, and I didn't really think about what we would do together after the paperwork was signed and the check cleared the bank. I just figured I'd continue working with her, and at some point, she would tell me what she enjoys doing, and what she would rather not do.

Still, in other cases, the answer is quite simple: If you've found yourself with a very senior horse, a companion-only horse, or a horse that for any reason is considered "pasture-sound" only, you don't really need to choose an occupation for your horse.

However, it is important that you come up with some plans for you and your horse so that you have a reason to spend time together. Your horse will likely get bored eating, roaming, and staring into the wind day after day. Likewise, you might find yourself mentally detaching from a horse that you don't actually interact with, which might lead you to question why you're pouring money into something you don't even play with.

You don't have to have a specific, detailed, or even well-thought out plan for what you and your horse are going to accomplish together, but you do need to have some basic idea of what you're going to do today, tomorrow, and even next week.

This section and the following section are intended to help you discover and understand what you and your horse could potentially accomplish together.

The following chapters will help you appreciate the scope of what you and your horse can do. Before you decide what activities you want to try, what type of training you want to invest in, and start shopping for an instructor, it's a good idea to get a general idea of what is within the realm of possibility. I encourage every horse person to try out as many equine disciplines and activities as they can, but at the same time, we all need to recognize what is and what isn't a good idea for long-term success.

Therefore, let's get started by arranging our hopes and dreams into a set of realistic goals and steps to take along the way.

Chapter 1: What Do You Want to Do?

What do *you* want to do in the equine world? This is actually a really big question because everything else hinges on the answer to this question.

Most people have a sort of "bucket list" for things they want to accomplish with horses. As a completely horse-obsessed teenager, I compiled the following list, which I titled in very large, all-capital letters "HORSE THINGS I NEED TO DO." The list is as follows:

- Own a horse
- Have a horse on my own property
- Jump a 3-foot course
- Gallop bareback
- Ride a gaited horse
- Try carriage driving
- Take reining lessons
- Ride a horse through the mountains
- Win a ribbon for riding a dressage test
- Ride in a parade
- Go on a cattle drive
- Train a green horse
- Take dressage lessons from a big name trainer
- Teach riding lessons
- Gain confidence
- Have fun

As a horse-crazed teenager, I had friends who were also horse-crazed teenagers. One friend had a list that was a little more specific. It's been many years, so I don't have her exact list memorized, but I remember sitting in the common room at our lesson barn thinking, "Am I doing this whole horse thing wrong?" Her goals were a lot more organized than mine:

Achievement	When
Qualify for State Finals on the local hunter/jumper circuit	This year
Intern at Hunterdon	Application due 1/1
Compete in Maclays*	All qualifying points by 8/31 1998
Compete in Medals**	All qualifying points by 8/31 1998
Olympics	2012

*This is the familiar name for the The National Horsemanship Championship for the ASPCA Alfred B. Maclay Trophy— the most prestigious competition for Junior hunter/jumper riders

** The nickname for the Dover Saddlery/USEF Hunter Seat Medal Final – another elite competition for Junior hunter/jumper riders

I share these two lists as fantastic examples of how different everyone's response can be when asked, "What do you want to do?" Even in my younger years, I wanted to try as many different things as possible. Meanwhile, my talented friend was working on the finer details of starting her professional career.

Unfortunately, I lost contact with my friend when she moved away, but I truly hope she was able to accomplish many of the things on her list. I've checked off most of my list, but I still have a couple things left to try.

I highly encourage you to write your own equine bucket list. When you do, be sure to look beyond the words on the page and consider what's between the lines.

Let's look at my list again. Only one of those goals is competition-related. That indicates that my passion wasn't in winning ribbons and gaining recognition, but exploring my skills and abilities when riding and working with horses. I didn't have a particular timeline. There's no white-knuckle discipline or sense of urgency. Just some cool stuff to do with horses before I lose the ability to work with them.

On the other hand, my friend had very specific goals and due dates to motivate her. From her list, she could actually plot exactly what horse shows she needed to enter in order to gain the correct amount of points to qualify for the next step in the process. As a result, she was incredibly focused in every interaction with her horse. She took multiple lessons a week, worked at the barn to help pay off board, and attended every relevant clinic she could to get both education and exposure among the horse community. Her goals were professional, while mine were recreational.

Your own goals are going to be personal to you and your current level of experience, and there are no wrong answers. Be honest with yourself – you might be shocked to discover that what you truly want out of your interactions with horses is a little different than what you had expected. For the longest time, I was convinced that I would be a professional rider and trainer. But I don't like going to horse shows, and I definitely lack the discipline to ride for hour after hour, day after day. I have the skill and talent to accomplish professional status, but I don't particularly want to put in the work.

Let your passion guide this list, not your well-rehearsed answers to questions about why you work with horses. Think about what you really want to do, not what you should do or what others expect you to do. You don't have to be the best equestrian in the whole wide world. Instead, try aiming to be the most *satisfied* equestrian in the whole wide world.

Take your time. You might even want to keep a journal on the topic, as you may find your interests and goals change over time. If you've never taken a jump, a three-foot course may sound pretty cool. But after you've held your breath in terror over a few crossrails, you might re-evaluate that particular goal.

Be honest, be completely passionate, and don't rush your decision-making process. However, bear in mind that identifying what you want to do with horses will dictate how and what you do with your horse for all of your remaining days together. And that can be an absolutely magical thing.

Chapter 2 : What Does Your Horse Want to Do?

Your horse is an important part of this equation as well. While we like to think we can "make" our horses do anything, the truth of the matter is that everything we do successfully with our horses is based on mutual agreement. This is why we work so hard to build that dynamic working relationship described in the last section.

You'll want to build on this relationship to keep it healthy; therefore, I recommend creating goals and ideas of concepts you would like to work on. You want every moment you spend with your horse to be enjoyable, and that means learning to ride, drive, or handle your horse correctly, so that you are aware of how to encourage the best performance out of you and your horse. This will help you build an even better relationship as you work together, but even more importantly, it's fantastic for both of you, physically. You'll both build muscles, balance, confidence, and skills that can be beneficial in other areas of your life as well. Additionally, having a "job" will help your horse maintain his sanity, as he has something to think about besides mischief-making and pestering his buddies.

Your horse cannot specifically tell you what he wants to do; however, you can look at his resume to see what he might apply for. In my book, *Finding Your First Horse : How to Buy a Horse without Losing Your Mind (or Money)*, we review the process of selecting a horse to do a certain job. If you have a very specific goal, such as competing in the Olympics or working with cattle, you can save yourself a lot of pain by choosing a horse who has natural aptitude in those areas. However, if you're more interested in having fun and trying different things, you'll likely find yourself with what we call an "all-arounder."

Your horse's breed might say a lot about their skills and talents. Thoroughbreds, for example, are generally bred for speed and agility. Quarter Horses, Paints, Pintos, Appaloosas, and other stock breeds value traits like sturdy conformation, quick-mindedness, and versatility.

Similarly, your horse's conformation might say a lot about the things that make them happy. The length of their legs compared to their body, the angle of their shoulder, the build of their hindquarters, and even the positioning of their neck to their back can contribute to how well-suited a horse is for a particular task.

That being said, most horses are perfectly comfortable performing at lower levels of nearly every equine sport. Always double-check with your vet to ensure that it is safe for your horse and to understand what limitations or risks they might encounter physically, but most horses have the potential to be quite versatile.

It's just that pesky thing where they have thoughts and opinions, and maybe they just don't want to do that job. Every once in a while, a horse will absolutely put a hoof down when it comes to trying certain things. The bravest horse I ever met, who competed successfully and cheerfully in CCI3 Star FEI Three Day Eventing competitions (just a step down from Olympic level competition) more or less refused to do anything but jump big scary things and move effortlessly through the complex movements of a high level dressage test, to the point where he would stop in his tracks and not budge if asked to do something he found ridiculous.

Your horse will make it very obvious if they do not enjoy the task you have put before them. If he trips over or runs through obstacles, he's not a jumper. If his fastest speed is a good-natured lope, he's not a contesting horse. If he can't bear to be in the general vicinity of a cow, he's not a cattle horse.

If you're not immediately certain what you want to do with your horse, take the time to try as many different sports and activities as possible. However, pay attention to your horse's reaction to each new thing you try. Do his ears perk up, steps seem lighter, and you feel that shift into performance mode when you do certain things? Or does he balk, throw it into reverse gear, and have a tantrum when you ask him to give something a whirl?

While it may seem dramatic to us as humans, either of these reactions are his way of telling you whether he enjoys a particular task or dreads it. A certain amount of persuasion may be required to get your horse to try new things in the first place. After all, they are very large prey animals who like to avoid confrontation and things that are difficult— but once that initial resistance is overcome, you'll get a very clear picture of whether your horse was born for this or doesn't ever need to try it again.

Chapter 3 : What Is Realistic for Both of You?

There are two very important words in the title of this chapter: "realistic" and "both."

When deciding what types of activities you'd like to explore with your horse, you need to consider the following words:

- Should
- Could
- Would

We know what your wants are as well as those of your horse. But now it's time to consider the reality of your situation. You'll want to find those magical crossroads where you and your horse can be happy working together regularly. Unfortunately, this means having to be honest with yourself in the face of your loftiest dreams.

I encourage you to consider this more as an exercise in looking for amazing opportunities than a chance to have your dreams squashed. You might find yourself drifting into the headspace of, "Well, since we can't do xyz..." but this is counter-productive. Instead of thinking of this as an exercise in what you *won't* be doing, consider it a positive way of understanding what you and your horse *can* accomplish together.

To keep honest to yourself and your horse's needs, ask yourself these questions:

- *What should my horse and I do together?* With this question, you are identifying what is physically possible for both of you. Horses and humans alike have limits as to what they can do. Not all humans can climb mountains without supplemental oxygen. Not all humans can do complex mental math. Not all humans can play concert piano. No matter how hard they try, the aptitude simply isn't there. However, many humans can hike up a hill, balance their bank account, and tap out "Chopsticks" on a keyboard. You and your horse may not be ideal candidates for the Olympics, but what if you make your goal a little less strenuous, and aim for ruling the world in the 2'3" Class?

- **What *could* my horse and I accomplish together?** This question builds off the last one. If we take Olympic qualification off the table, what are some opportunities that come into focus as very real possibilities? For those who enjoy the social aspect of the horsey world, perhaps you can join a local group that practices certain activities together, such as hunting, Gymkhana, or Trail riding. Maybe you can join a breed or sport organization that has state, regional, and world level showing that can provide you with endless goals both at home and in competition.

- **What would I be *willing to do* to make these goals happen?** This question is formatted a bit differently. It's an uncomfortable question, but extremely important to the equation of figuring out how you and your horse are going to proceed together. Dreams are wonderful, and you should nurture your dreams. However, dreams do not come true without a big scoop of hard work and humility. Whatever your goals are, you will be working towards them every time you work with your horse. Are you willing to make sacrifices in time and money so that you can reach your dreams? Are your goals important enough for you to prioritize them? Do you have the financial ability to invest in supplies, trainers, show fees, travel expenses, and so on?

As you read these questions, please remember— the occupation you choose for you and your horse doesn't have to be measured quantitatively. There's absolutely nothing wrong with saying, "My goal for my horse and I is to enjoy ourselves and always end our sessions together on a good note."

Furthermore, you'll want to recognize that every big goal has many little goals leading up to it. Your "big goal" might be to jump a three-foot course, but on the way to that goal, both you and your horse need to learn how to trot and canter over poles and become adept at jumping smaller fences first. Depending on where you and your horse are in your training and skill level when you meet, that three-foot course might be something you do the week you bring him home or a few years in the future.

It is very appropriate to ask yourself these questions frequently, especially if you are working with a young horse, or you are inexperienced. You may find that you have to pivot in your plans from time to time. Since learning is not linear, especially when both parties involved are autonomous beings, there will be setbacks. You will change your mind. Your horse will turn up lame, or you'll feel unwell.

Remember that the only standards to which you are accountable are your own. Your primary responsibility in working with your horse in any capacity is to the physical and mental well-being of both of you. Sure, it hurts when dreams don't come true, but there is a lot to be celebrated about recognizing when you've reached the top of your potential. Another horse might have the talent you need, or you might find that both of you excel in a completely surprising area of equine sports. There is no rush, and no need to push either the horse or yourself past your physical, mental, and emotional comfort zone.

Everyone wants to achieve certain goals with their horses, and that is both healthy and admirable. We all need to have an idea of what we want to do with our horses every day to keep us healthy and happy, even if that plan is as simple as just having fun together. I believe that maintaining physical and mental health of both parties should be the primary goal of any equine-human relationship.

I also believe that varies greatly between each equine and human. The goals I have for Belle are not the same as those for Red, just as my goals are not the same as many of my barn mates. What matters most, in my opinion, is that everyone is on the same page when it comes to accomplishing various feats, which can help your relationship with your horse become something you cherish for a very long time.

It might seem a little out of the realm of logic to emphasize the importance of the relationship between a horse and a human and take their feelings into consideration when it comes to choosing what you two accomplish together. However, my own opinion is that if you have the opportunity to build a good working relationship with your horse, why wouldn't you at least give it a try?

I find this especially true in the case of first-time horse owners. You have found yourself in an amazing situation, wherein you are able to connect and have a meaningful relationship with another sentient creature. Even if you never get on his back, you can enjoy each other's company. Even if he is a highly trained professional discouraged from snuggling random cute things, you and your horse can build mutual respect for each other.

It's not unrealistic to enjoy the presence of another living creature. We do it with dogs and cats all the time. We tend to view horses through a different lens since they are historically work animals. They're also very large and don't snuggle on sofas very well. But they are still very much living creatures, and if you choose to share your life and paycheck with one, why not enjoy every possible moment?

Author's Anecdote- Red's Very Specific List of Demands

I picked up Red when he was four years old. As of this writing, he is sixteen years old. It's fair to say we know each other very well.

When I first brought him home, my goal was to get him healthy enough to be ridden. Once it became apparent that he was going to be just fine, my goal was to canter him under saddle. He hadn't cantered for a rider since his days on the track, and no one was sure he even could. After he demonstrated he had a very nice canter, I came up with more long-term goals for our partnership.

I wanted to train him to jump a two-foot fence and perform a First Level dressage test. On the scale of difficulty in the general equine world, these are pretty basic requests. But at the end of the day, that's all I wanted to do, and that's all he should do, with his various health problems.

Moreover, Red demonstrated to me very early in our relationship that he wasn't super motivated to accomplish much. Instead of snapping to attention and doing groundwork with focus, he wanted to cuddle and play with the barn cats. He wandered off when anything cute and fuzzy walked by the arena like a dog, goat, or small child. We would have moments of work that were absolutely brilliant, but other days I would practically be begging him to go forward. The inconsistency in our work together was maddening.

So, why did I keep working with him? Because of his amazing calmness. Even as a racehorse fresh off the track, he demonstrated great mental capacity for problem solving. He's a big horse, and the barn at which we were boarding was pretty small. He often got tangled in things in the aisleway, and always stopped, carefully extracted himself, and went back to standing patiently.

Therefore, imagine my surprise when one day I arrived at the barn to a wild-eyed, rearing chestnut beast my barn owner described as "stark-raving mad." My snuggly Thoroughbred had blossomed into a large, equine-shaped ball of energy and emotion. I was concerned about his health, but I was also very worried that my mild-mannered horse had finally become the "brainless racehorse" stereotype overnight.

In my attempt to check him over in his stall, he shoved past me and took off at a dead gallop. I was absolutely petrified. Was he gone forever? Would he make it to the road and lose his footing? I cursed my extensive knowledge of equine behavior as every possible worst case scenario flooded my mind.

But, here's what actually happened: Red took off out of the barn. He ran the length of the pasture fence, which bordered the woods. He was angry about the tree branches poking him, so he bucked and galloped full out to get back out of the woods. He pranced around the parking lot for a bit, then found a patch of grass and started eating. I walked up to him, clipped the lead line to his halter, let him catch his breath, and it was just like nothing had happened.

Suddenly, it clicked : this was the utter essence of Red. Sure, he had occasional bursts of energy, but he didn't have the attitude to sustain it. A horse that competes needs to have the energy and determination to do well. If I took this horse to a show, we might have one amazing class, and then he'd be busy trying to snuggle with a pony. Red didn't want to go-go-go; he just wanted to have a little fun once in a while.

I took him to one show to prove this theory, and I was right on the money with my assessment. We plodded around the warm-up ring. Then he realized there were lots of strangers there and got excited. I took him in one class, where he stood at the fence and whinnied for most of it, followed by several very rapid, unbalanced canter circles. It was a Walk/Trot Equitation Class. There is no cantering in these classes, but there was also neither walk nor trot in my horse at that moment.

Once the class was over, he decided he wanted to hang out by the trailer and eat grass with his buddy. I tried tacking him up for another class, but he wasn't interested in listening to me. It just wasn't his gig, and since it's not mine either, I didn't see a reason to force the issue.

Now that the mystery of what my horse wanted to do was resolved, we started having more fun, which resulted in more productive work sessions. Sometimes I'd clip a lead rope on his halter, and we'd walk the trails on the property together. Sometimes I'd hop on bareback and just walk around. Other times, we'd pick up a particular skill, like lead changes, leg yield, or extended trot.

But most importantly, I learned what my buddy likes and doesn't like. He will not permit anyone to ride him in a place where he eats. That means no galloping across the pasture, or even doing pony rides in a paddock where he's been turned out before. He'll get very upset and bounce up and down if anyone tries to ride him in his play area. He will specifically tell me when he needs to be lunged before I ride, and when I can just hop on by pinning his ears at me and dancing in place when I try to get on. Sometimes, we'll be working on a particular skill, and he'll decide he needs to canter a few laps as a palette cleanser.

Likewise, I share my requests with him. When I say, "Pony Ride," he knows that I'm deep in my feelings or anxious, and that I just need him to plod around on a long rein while I gather myself. Once I'm ready to work, I'll pick up the contact on the reins, and he'll shift his gait into a more forward, ready-to-go stride.

I can happily say that every ride is a good ride because we can communicate. We have fights, but we're able to understand what the other is trying to "say" through their behavior. I'm willing to engage in more fights with him because we are able to work through them more easily than I can with a horse I don't know as well. We can find mutual ground, build into new skills, and have productive fights because we have worked together in the spirit of understanding.

PART 2 : AN INTRODUCTION TO EQUINE SPORTS AND ACTIVITIES

Many of you might have read the last section about goal-setting and thought, "Gee, that's great, but I'm not sure what I want to do." You might be new to horses, or you've never really considered dabbling in anything but your current sport.

Therefore, the second half of this book is dedicated towards helping you decide which sports and activities you and your horse may want to try. We'll take a look at various disciplines and the different types and styles of riding you can explore.

I want to mention that this is in no way to be considered a complete guide to everything horse-related. There are plenty of sports that don't regularly receive the attention they deserve, either because they are very niche— such as vaulting and circus trick riding— or overlap with other activities— for example, war reenactment riders. I don't want to diminish the skill and effort displayed by those equestrians because I admire all equine activities equally. However, I wanted to create a very basic outline of some of the most popular activities with the hopes that it will provide new equestrians with enough details to spark their interest to explore further.

To get the most out of this part of the book, I encourage you to read all of the sections first. Make a note of what intrigues you. Then head to the "Resources" section to find websites that will lead you to more information on each discipline.

For others, you may have a degree of certainty as to your path with your horse. You might be taking lessons with an instructor whom you admire greatly. You might think this part of the book has nothing to offer you. I still recommend you read this part of the book so you can gain greater insight into the vastness of the equestrian world. There may come a time when your interests or abilities change, or you might find yourself getting into a rut with your current training and need to find a little excitement. Just like humans, horses can get bored of doing the same thing over and over. Mixing things up once in a while can be very beneficial for helping you and your horse find new ways to problem solve and achieve results as a team.

As you read through the following sections, don't be afraid to think, "I'd like to try that." Even professional equestrians swap horses so they can learn new things about how horses move and perform. Therefore, without further ado, let's dive into some of the many exciting possibilities for equestrian enjoyment.

SECTION 1 : THE ENGLISH DISCIPLINES

There are two main types of saddles in the equestrian world: English, also known as hunt seat, and Western. "English" is so called because it directly descends from the manner of riding developed and popularized in England. The saddles were designed to provide mounted hunters and cavalry with an open seat, which would allow for flexibility and movement when galloping over fences and covering terrain that included hills, valleys, and streams.

In English riding, great emphasis is put upon the rider's position and effectiveness, known as "equitation". Their heels are down, their chest open, and their spine straight. But, appearances aren't everything. These disciplines involve a very specific and direct form of contact between the rider and the horse that requires a nuanced center of balance, a soft, following arm that connects directly with the horse's mouth via the bit, and an appearingly super-straight, tall spine. It's actually the result of fully activated abdominal muscles.

Hunt seat saddles are often very minimalist, especially jumping saddles. The panels are thin, the seats flat, and padding at the knees and thighs, known as "rolls" is for bridging the gap between the rider and horse's anatomy rather than providing comfort. The stirrups, known as irons, are connected to the saddle by thin stirrup leathers, which look impossibly thin and fragile. In truth, there's generally not a whole lot of equipment between the horse and rider.

Therefore, riders who are starting out with the English disciplines often feel very loose in the saddle and unstable. Developing a secure seat is the key to giving you a feeling of safety and helping you stay out of the horse's way when he moves.

However, it takes a lot of practice and confidence to feel secure. Many riders who switch to English disciplines after riding a different style for a while report feeling like their legs are swinging around wildly. Your first time in an English saddle, you might feel your spine try to curl into a comfortable fetal position. Your legs might grip the horse in terror, and your arms and shoulders may clench as you grip the reins in two white-knuckled hands.

You may feel so vulnerable and imperiled that you give up right then and there. Allow me to assure you that every single rider has felt completely insecure at some point in an English saddle.

I recall my first English lesson. I had been riding Western pleasure for a year, and it wasn't really my thing. I didn't dislike it, but I wanted to try this jumping thing, which meant changing saddles. My first ride in an English saddle was on the same horse I had ridden for my very first lesson years before. I had long since gained enough skill to ride other horses, but my instructor assured me I wanted to ride the easiest horse possible.

We never made it out of a walk. The minute my seat touched the unfamiliar saddle, my legs forgot where they were supposed to go. My heels shot up in the air. My hands couldn't figure out the short reins, and my neck immediately stiffened in fear, taking the rest of my body with it. I sat up there in solid fear until my instructor asked if we could please end the lesson early or switch to a Western saddle.

I did neither. My father moaned about spending money for me to walk around in circles for an hour, but I was slowly gaining my balance. I was finding my place in the saddle and learning how to move my hips with the horse instead of bracing against the natural movement of his back. Soon, I was trotting, then cantering, and eventually, I was doing that jumping thing that had intrigued me in the first place.

Today, I like to share this story with my own students because I believe it's important to know that we all learn in different ways. For some people, sitting in an English saddle feels quite natural, especially if you have a stocky horse and a saddle that fits you well. But if you're a smaller person on a narrow horse or in a saddle that doesn't fit you well, you may feel wildly insecure.

As you read the following descriptions of some popular hunt seat disciplines, I want you to keep in mind that there are different levels of all of these sports. Everyone starts over ground poles before they go over fences. Everyone learns how to halt and salute at X before they do canter pirouettes. Being a beginner equestrian is nothing to be ashamed of; in fact, you should feel very proud of yourself for having the gumption to strap yourself to a 1,000-pound prey animal in the first place.

Now, trot on to discover the different things you can do with an English saddle and practice!

Chapter 1: Riding on the Flat

Champion Hunter Under Saddle. Hunt Seat Equitation. Open English Equitation. Handy Hunter. Working Hunter. What do all of these mean?

When researching the various forms of English riding online, you'll likely find terms like these, especially when looking at various show bills, or a training barn may proudly enthuse about their skills in these areas. It sounds great, but what do all of these words translate to in terms of riding?

English classes are broken into two sub-categories: over fences and on the flat. As the name implies, "over fences" means jumping, as in jumping over fences. Flat classes mean the exact opposite— there are no fences, and the class takes place on flat ground.

There are two different areas of focus in English riding. The first is the horse. A hunt seat horse should have an open shoulder, a long, even stride, a steady temperament, and precise transitions between gaits.

The second focus is the rider. The term "equitation" has long been thought to refer only to a rider's position, but the meaning of the word goes a lot deeper. Yes, a magnificently lowered heel, a steady seat, and that ramrod straight spine are important, but true equitation involves riders finding a position that is most effective for a particular horse. Equitation does not mean shoving your body into a position and locking it there. In fact, locking your body so it doesn't move is the last thing your horse wants.

True equitation involves a secure, balanced rider who is able to coax a stunning performance out of their horse without obvious kicking, yanking, and cursing. The horse seems to respond to psychic cues from the rider to change direction, transition from one gait to another, and even perform complicated patterns without either party appearing to put a whole lot of effort into it. As a trainer once explained to me, "Equitation is when you just happen to do everything right, and you look amazing doing it."

So, what's with the many iterations of hunter flat options? Essentially, they all boil down to the same type of riding. Hunt seat horses are expected to have a long, low, and relaxed frame. "Even" and "steady" are the two buzzwords commonly associated with the hunter ring. Some hunters may focus strictly on rail work, meaning they ride around the exterior of an arena at walk, trot, canter, and sometimes hand gallop, usually with at least one change of rein— show speak for "change direction." Other classes require riders to complete a pattern which can include a variety of options such as making a circle, changing leads in the canter, weaving between cones, and even hopping over small jumps.

You don't have to show in order to enjoy hunter-style riding. You can work on creating a smooth, even, steady gait at walk, trot, and canter from the comfort of your own barn. Exercises such as ground poles will help establish balance in both yourself and your horse. You'll want to concentrate on encouraging your horse to move through his entire body, keeping his spine long and loose from his poll (where the spine connects to the skull between his ears) to his tail.

Hunter flat riding is as much about creating an elegant aesthetic as encouraging and sustaining movement that is balanced and regulated. This sort of consistency isn't natural for humans or horses; therefore, while you might think hunt seat is "easier" than disciplines that include a course or a test, your core muscles and glutes might beg to differ after your first lesson. That's what makes flat riding a key component to all of the English disciplines, and a basis for the next several sports we'll discuss.

Chapter 2 : Dressage

Somewhere along the line, dressage gained a reputation for being the snootiest equine discipline. Maybe it's because the sport itself requests absolute perfection from the horse and rider. Maybe it's because of the pristine white breeches, black tail coats, and satin top hats that used to be worn for high level competition. I personally think it's the fact that top level champion dressage horses cost more than my mortgage, but that might be just a touch of jealousy oozing out.

Dressage is definitely my thing. I've always wanted to learn dressage, and once I finally found a program that fit my needs, I immediately stopped doing everything else so I could learn more. Fear not– I'm not going to proselytize on the topic of "horse dancing." Though I personally believe everyone should try it, I appreciate that some people prefer a sport that has black and white versions of success and failure.

Dressage is, for lack of a better word, multi-dimensional. Some may say "impossible," because it truly is impossible to get a perfect score on a dressage test. However, if you step back from the competition aspect, it's really a matter of developing an exquisite relationship with your horse and an appreciation for movement. It really is dancing, with a horse and rider as partners.

A dressage test consists of a variety of movements. These movements can include walk, trot, and canter at various tempos, in which the horse "collects," or contains energy for little forward movement, or "extends," by moving forward expressively. These gaits are performed along the border of the arena, in circles of various sizes, or in serpentine patterns. There are lateral movements in which the horse moves sideways towards and away from the outer borders of the dressage ring, rapid-fire lead changes, and even feats of balance and poise, as in the piaffe, where a horse trots in place for several strides in a row.

Dressage tests are ridden in an arena marked with letters. These letters are placed at regular metered intervals along the outside walls, and along the centerline of the arena as well, though most arenas don't have markers in the middle of the dirt.

It is alleged that these letters originated from the markers that indicated where individuals of importance, such as the king's courier, would expect to receive their horses in Germany's Imperial Court. This certainly seems a reasonable explanation, but generations of riders since have used various mnemonics to remember the seemingly random selection of letters that appear every few meters in a dressage ring. The distance between letters depends on whether the test is ridden in a standard arena or a small arena, which in turn depends on the level of test being ridden.

The levels begin with tests that explore the horse and rider aptitude at skills that are taught early in training such as walking, halting, and trotting. Each subsequent level introduces movements that require greater fitness and ability to execute, with movements occurring faster and with more difficulty in transitioning from one to another.

But here's the catch: you're being judged on how well you do it. According to the United States Dressage Federation website, the following qualities are top priority in dressage:

- *Gaits: The freedom and regularity.*
- *Impulsion: Desire to move forward, elasticity of the steps, suppleness of the back, and engagement of the hindquarters.*
- *Submission: The horse's attention and confidence, lightness and ease of movements, acceptance of the bridle, lightness of the forehand, and straightness.*
- *Rider's position and seat.*
- *Rider's correctness and effect of the aid.*

When I say dressage "requests perfection," I mean that each movement is scored from 1-10, with 1 meaning it wasn't good at all to 10 being "excellent." The points are then totaled up and calculated as a percentage of the total possible points. If the movements in a test totalled 100 points, for example, earning 60 out of 100 points would translate into a test score of 60%.

Judges are also encouraged to write notes to explain their scoring, so that riders have an idea of what they can work on in the future. Perfection isn't expected at all; in fact, scores of 60-70% are considered proficient enough for the duo to move up to the next level.

So, why participate in a sport where you can't possibly achieve perfection? For me, the best part of dressage is that I'm only as good as I am at any given moment. It really is a matter of doing the best you can and seeing how your best in this exact test compares to the test you rode yesterday, last week, or last year. Each ride we have is different because each day is different. The horse may be feeling grumpy. The rider might have a stiff neck from sleeping poorly the night before. Still, they perform the movements to the best of their ability in hopes that they will continue to grow in their partnership. In my opinion, it's poetic and affirming.

Plus, there are practical applications to dressage. The sport was created by Greek military riders to display their uniform riding mastery. Other military legions around the world picked up the training as a way to ensure all horses and riders were able to develop to the same standard of athleticism and cunning when going into battle as well. The Imperial Spanish Riding School of Vienna, which was created in 1572, is perhaps one of the most famous examples of classical dressage riding still in existence today. The famous Lipizzaner Stallions train at this facility and demonstrate the discipline as it was intended to be ridden in the Renaissance era. A mounted militia isn't as important to the modern world as it was many centuries ago; therefore, dressage has developed into a test of creating smooth, seamless, cooperative movement. The rider's cues to the horse should be nearly invisible, and the horse should respond in agreement. Precision in execution of each movement leads to higher skills.

This type of training can benefit any horse and rider pair. Dressage encourages horse and rider to use all of their muscles simultaneously to propel them with grace and accuracy. In fact, I liken dressage more to yoga than dancing since the key to success is being able to activate and relax all of your body parts at once. Every shift of balance and pressure from the rider from a squeeze of the thigh to a nudge of the heel, has a different meaning, and yet, the rider must breathe and be at ease. As my trainer has mentioned many times, dressage is the art of turning as little action as possible into the most beautiful movement possible.

The top complaint I hear is that dressage is boring. I can see this point of view because to the untrained eye, nothing is really happening. But the act of riding dressage, when one puts in the effort to assist their horse in moving comfortably and correctly, while maintaining a peaceful and cooperative connection, is an act that requires almost zen-like patience and a full admission of your own fallibility.

At the higher levels of dressage, riders use a specialized dressage saddle. These are typically black, deep seated saddles with long flaps that extend under the rider's thigh and calf. The goal is to allow the rider to position themselves in a way that permits them to follow the movement of the muscles in the horse's back, increasing the sensitivity of the seat. This means that even small amounts of pressure from the rider become "invisible" cues, leading to the illusion that horse and rider are working together via psychic connection.

However, you don't need any specific equipment (or any equipment at all) to work on harmony and forward motion at all gaits. I encourage every equestrian to try the basics of dressage, as it has the potential to break down a lot of resistance that you and your horse may be encountering while learning another discipline. Consider it couples counseling for you and your horse!

Chapter 3 : Jumping

You'd be hard pressed to find someone who isn't impressed with the aerial feats of riders and horses soaring over obstacles. For a brief moment, it's as if Pegasus manifested, and flying on the back of a noble steed is a real possibility. Defying gravity, they propel above the ground, then gracefully touch down on the other side.

Or not. Navigating a large, opinionated beast around a set course of obstacles which must be taken in a specific order, often within a specific time limit, is an activity with little room for error. If a horse doesn't feel comfortable jumping, they'll stop before they have to. Most of the time, the rider's momentum will carry them over the fence without the horse, resulting in at least a dirty face and bruised ego. Horses can also misjudge the height or distance they need to jump and clip a rail or stumble upon landing. There's also the chance of the dreaded rotational fall, in which the horse essentially somersaults head-first over a fence. Jumping is dangerous, but many riders agree that the feeling of flying far outweighs the fear of falling.

A common misconception is that jumping is easy. The horse does all the work, right? While it's true that the horse is in charge of carrying himself and the rider over the fence, the rider is responsible for helping the horse get to and over the fence as safely and correctly as possible. In jumping, the term "correct" refers to maintaining enough momentum in between fences to propel the duo over each obstacle and finding a good "distance" or spot from which the horse can take off.

The goal is to set your horse up so that the span and apex of the jump give him enough room to clear the obstacle so that he doesn't hit a rail or bring down a fence with an errant hoof. One of my trainers explained it, "The horsey flies, but the horsey won't fly well if you don't ride well."

Jumping is difficult, but also incredibly rewarding. The first time you pop over a cross-rail, you get that miniscule moment of being weightless combined with the knowledge that you just made a horse fly. The adrenaline rush is exquisite, and the amount of mental and physical prowess required to get through a course well is a challenge many riders thoroughly enjoy.

There are several different types of jumping as well, each of which brings a different perspective to the concept of getting a horse over an obstacle.

Hunter Jumpers

As an extension of hunt seat riding on the flat, hunter jumpers are expected to go around a course of fences with the same steady, even stride.

Generally speaking, the jump courses for hunter rounds aren't super complex. The jumps are set at heights that typically range from eighteen inches to three feet, six inches. Jumps increase in height in increments of three inches, so a 2'0" rider will progress to a 2'3" course, and so on. The most common fence type is a regular vertical, or a fence that consists of two standards and a pole. Oxers, or obstacles that are both wide and high, are not uncommon in higher levels of competition and can include verticals set closely together to form a single jump effort or solid-appearing objects such as rolltops, coops, and flower boxes. I've included more information on hunter courses in the "Resources" section, if you'd like to explore more.

The most common course design, especially for lower levels, includes two outside lines and two fences on the inside diagonal line, meaning the pattern resembles a figure-8. There are a few deviations from this standard, of course, but the point of the course is to demonstrate the horse's ability to present a forward, even, and balanced stride on both canter leads, including at least one lead change. "Lead" is the term used for the leg that leads when the horse is cantering- the inside leg should be the one that strikes the ground first when the horse is cantering. A lead change, therefore, means changing direction, and thus, changing which leg is leading.

Over the fences, the horses should present themselves as sharp, strong, and capable. This ideal includes high, tightly tucked knees, and a rounded spine that indicates the horse is using his entire body to clear the obstacle. The rider's goal is to ensure an even and exact number of strides between the fences, with the horse presenting a uniform athletic effort over each fence.

Equitation is highly emphasized in hunter jumpers. The rider is expected to maintain a soft, following hand, with open shoulder angles, and an open hip that allows the horse to use his entire body to power over the fence. Heels should be down and aligned with the hip to provide balance and stability through the arch of the jump. To all appearances, the rider should simply be floating along on the horse's back, going with the motion instead of interfering.

The overall concept to keep in mind for hunters is "minimalism." The riders dress in plain black or navy jackets with beige or white breeches, tall black dress boots, and hair neatly hidden in a hunt cap. Saddles and bridles are plain, and if a saddle pad is used, it is generally plain white. The idea is to remove all distinctive features so the judge can focus on the movement and performance of the horse and rider. I'd like to add that, despite what you may see on television and in movies, hunter jumpers don't wear the hunt coat every single time they ride- only in the show ring.

Those coats are expensive, hard to clean, and often super hot and stuffy, like a suit jacket. Most riders don't enjoy wearing them unless it's absolutely necessary.

Regardless of whether you wear a coat or even consider entering a show ring, training for hunter jumper courses can be a great way to build fitness in you and your horse. One way in which hunters achieve this fitness is by schooling– what we call our at-home practice rides– over gymnastics or jump sets in which each obstacle immediately precedes the next. This builds core muscle for horse and human and develops the roundness and athleticism required to snap those knees high and arch roundly over each fence. I've put some examples in the "Resources" section so you can see for yourself if this is something you and your pony would like to try.

Show Jumping

Many people are introduced to show jumping via the Summer Olympics as it is one of the few equestrian sports that is regularly televised. In 2021, Olympic Show Jumping received an extra dose of attention, as rock legend Bruce Springsteen's daughter, Jessica Springsteen, rode on the silver medal-winning United States team. People who had never really considered the world of equestrian sports were suddenly made aware of a sport in which people willingly rode their horses at top speed towards and over weird-looking obstacles measuring over five feet in height and up to six feet, five inches in width. On top of that, the horse and rider team who completes the course fastest with the fewest poles down wins. Even non-horsey people can be sucked into rooting for a particular duo as they watch horse and rider teams charge boldly at behemoth jumps.

Not all show jumping courses include fences over five feet, or 1.6 meters now that the Fédération Equestre Internationale (FEI) is officially using the metric system in course guides. Like any other sport, beginners start out over smaller fences, and as they gain comfort and ability at the sport, the fences become larger.

Some people think of show jumping as the "opposite" of hunters since hunter-jumpers focus on form and presence, while show jumpers aim for a clear round in which no fences or poles are pulled down when the horse goes over the jumps, in the fastest time. It doesn't really matter *how* a show jumper gets around the course or what their equitation looks like, just that they land the last fence alive and well.

Of course, that's a bit of a hyperbolic look at show jumpers, as they are fantastically athletic, with swiftness to carry them rapidly along the flat ground winding between the jumps. They have the agility to adjust their stride to spring high into the air and land gracefully over a dozen fences.

While hunter classes are designed to display a horse's athleticism through perfect repetition, a show jumping course requires the horse and rider to solve problems. This can include weird distances between fences, which can require adjusting your speed and tempo with each stride, tight turns, bending lines, and combination fences, in which the horse jumps a fence, has two or three strides to gather himself before the next fence of equal height, then one stride upon landing in order to prepare for the third fence in the group. Don't forget you're trying to jump them without knocking anything over. And do it faster than the last guy!

Show jumping looks hard because it is hard, and I'm pretty excited that it's finally getting national recognition. On the other hand, I imagine some people find it discouraging that you can't just start show jumping. First, you need to learn how to ride, then get the basics of jumping under your belt, have the physical fitness required to contain 1,000 pounds of raw energy, holding it back and pushing it as needed in order to quickly get through a twisted, winding maze of fences. I'm afraid you aren't going to be show jumping in your first lesson. You can become a show jumper— just not overnight. Give it at least a few years.

However, the concepts involved in show jumping are fantastic for building athleticism and agility in any horse. One of my favorite exercises for any horse is to build a show jumping course out of poles laid on the ground. It doesn't actually have to make sense— the beauty of this exercise is that you are going to be adjusting your horse to remain balanced and forward even when taking impossibly tight turns and uneven distances. Doing this exercise at a walk is a great way to help horses loosen up and move forward at the walk, which is when most horses enjoy seeing how lazy we'll let them be. Red is famous for shuffling along at the walk until he trips, so I'll do this exercise at the trot first, then make him walk over poles until it occurs to him that he can pick up his feet just a little more.

If words like big, fast, and "whee!" are attractive to you, then you might be interested in learning more about show jumping opportunities in your area. I've included some links in the "Resources" section to help you get started.

Cross Country / Three Day Eventing

The terms "cross country" and "eventing" are often used interchangeably, though they don't quite mean the same thing. Cross country is one of the stages of three day eventing, which to complicate matters more is also known as "combined training," or "horse trials" as it combines three different activities into one competition.

Three day eventing is an equestrian sport that, as the name implies, takes part in three phases. At introductory levels, the three phases are completed in the same day, but at FEI and Olympic levels, the events take place on three separate days to allow horses and riders to recuperate between challenges.

Why three different sports in one? The goal of three day eventing is to demonstrate the athletic prowess of horse and rider. Essentially, this is the equine triathlon. Established as a sport back when the cavalry held demonstrations of their skills and capabilities, eventing has gone through many changes over the years; however, it remains a test of will, determination, talent, bravery, and yes, the ability to run fast and jump scary things.

The first event is dressage. The concept of dressage within the context of eventing is the same as that within dressage as a stand alone discipline: the horse and rider must convey the impression that they are silently, magically, and mysteriously dancing as one. Horse and rider pairs are scored on quality of gait, balance and suppleness in turns and transitions, collection and extension, engagement, and harmony between horse and rider.

The movements that are requested in the test are less based on classical dressage, but rooted in demonstrating the ability for horse and rider to communicate practically. Piaffe and passage are not part of eventing dressage; instead, you'll find plenty of transitions, circles, half-passes, collection and extension, and riding to and out of the halt.

Next is cross country... usually. There are different formats to different three day events depending on the size, the levels of competition included in the event, and the organization holding the show. Some smaller shows present stadium jumping as the second event. Larger events have road and tracks and steeplechase segments in which horses are asked to gallop across the countryside and sail over fences within a certain amount of time. The most popular version is the "short" event in which the second event asks horse and rider to gallop across open land, tree-lined trails, over bridges, through water, and more in the exciting cross country jumping round.

I encourage you to check out some of the videos included in the "Resources" section to gain a sense of how much bravery and athleticism is required of horse and rider in the upper levels of eventing. It's not the size of the fence that's as intimidating as the fact that each obstacle asks a lot of questions of the horse and rider. You may approach a jump in the middle of running up or down a hill, meaning your take off and landing are two different heights. You may jump off a bank into a pool of water, then jump another bank upwards out of the water. The obstacles are usually based on things you would find when galloping around your own backyard- logs, ditches, creeks, abandoned objects, walls, fences, or small houses. And each obstacle is just as solid as it looks with no room for error. It's easy to be intimidated by the potential for failure.

The last phase of three day eventing is stadium jumping. This is very similar to show jumping in that horse and rider are back in the ring, competing over a course of fences to see who has the clearest round in the fastest time. At this point, horse and rider are tired, running on the last vestiges of adrenaline, and potentially wondering if they could back track their decision making process to the moment when this sounded like a good idea. Still, they persevere by navigating a technically difficult course of jumps.

At the end of the three events, each pair's score is tallied, and the horse and rider with the fewest errors are declared the winners. That is a very simplistic explanation of how eventing scoring works, but explaining all of the various coefficients and penalty awards for each different format of eventing by each ruling committee is practically its own college major, let alone a book!

Is eventing for you? You will know. Just as it takes a very specific set of abilities to compete in a human triathlon, three day eventing requires training, discipline, and commitment, not to mention heaps and heaps of bravery. It is truly a sport in which each step must be calculated and purposeful, and both horse and rider must be able to deal with a variety of rapidly-changing scenarios. Accuracy is the key to success, along with the ability to adapt quite literally mid-stride to accommodate error or misjudgement. It requires an amount of skill and patience that I greatly admire.

There is great benefit in schooling outdoors, and over even small fences in strange places. Many riders have encountered a fallen tree while on a trail ride and had to make a quick decision about how to proceed. Furthermore, training for endurance and adaptability can benefit every horse and rider. That being said, I recommend you do any attempted eventing under the tutelage of a trained professional,because when things go wrong in eventing, they can be fatal.

But if that doesn't scare you off, there's very likely a cross country course near you just waiting for you to try it!

Field Hunting

You know those old paintings you see, of red-coated riders and stoic brown horses jumping over fences, hedges, and tearing through the woods after a pack of hound dogs? That's known as field hunting which is linked to more low-key versions of the sport such as hunter paces.

In the original sport, a group of riders mounted up to ceremoniously chase a fox across the countryside. The expectation was that the excursion would last all day. In fact, several riders are employed to help guide the hunting dogs through terrain that makes the sport even more fun and daring for the riders. At its root, this type of hunting was more of a social event between neighboring equestrians than a survivalist search for food, with traditions such as a pre-hunt breakfast and a post-hunt feast, along with several pit stops along the way for conviviality.

Historically speaking, only male riders were permitted to ride astride, with one leg on each side of the horse. Women rode "aside", or sidesaddle. In fact, riding astride as a female only became normalized in Western culture as recently as the 1930s! Today, there are quite a few riders who continue the tradition of riding sidesaddle, and in modern day riding, men are invited to ride aside as well.

Social implications of the sport aside, field hunting and its offshoot trials and paces are known for their good-natured social aspect, rather than serving as a staunch competition. Though some of these sports offer prizes and placement, most riders participate for the thrill of riding across the countryside and finding new and exciting obstacles to navigate over, around, and through.

Though the paintings from the 1800s depict a pack of riders heading at full-tilt, most field hunting involves a significant amount of walking and trotting, as the terrain and weather permit. Mud is a familiar factor, and hunters in the United States typically gather in the fall and winter months when there are fewer leaves on the trees. There may be a lot of standing around and waiting, especially if there are hounds involved. Some field gatherings offer different groups centered around skill level and comfort riding in the open, which allows each group to set a pace that works for everyone.

Still, the full-tilt thing does happen, and that's what makes the whole thing thrilling. The trees turn to a brownish-gray blur as you pick up speed, as you brace yourself against wind, rain, and the possibility of getting smacked in the face by twigs and low-hanging branches. The pursuit can last for a good stretch of time before the pack slows once again, but it won't be long until the hunt is back on.

"Hunting" at home is one of the most common activities among young equestrians, especially those with bold ponies and a large pasture, field, or trail system to explore on their own property. I have particularly fond memories of watching a bunch of kids in rubber boots hop on their ponies bareback to hunt through the woods for one of the barn cats, whose name just happened to be Foxy.

This is not to sound dismissive of hunting at all— in order to successfully participate, you need the bravery of a three day eventer, the endurance to stay on horseback for an entire day, the sense of adventure to purposefully get lost, and the skillful equitation that can help you ride through any potential mess. Then, add in the general excitement of the pack and the braying of the hounds, and you have an experience that will challenge every aspect of your equestrian knowledge.

What separates field hunting from trail riding or plain old-fashioned goofing off on a horse? There's a great deal of ceremony and tradition involved in hunting, and there are rules that give it an air of organization. But I suspect underneath all of the pomp and circumstance, we're all inclined to ride off into the sunset, regardless of whether we're in pursuit of a fox, a barn cat, or our own imagination. So, whether you join a local pack or invent one in your backyard, why not sneak in a little hunt now and again to test your bravery and horsemanship?

Hunt Seat in a Nutshell

Yes, that's a lot of information to take in at once. Just as Rome wasn't built in a day, no one has learned all of these disciplines and activities at once. Even three day eventers take three days to complete their phases.

Again, this information isn't intended to be taken as professional instruction but more as an inspiration as you and your horse work to find your stride together. Whether you're looking for new ways to play together at home or searching for a career that will put you on the track for professional status, these are a sample of some of the popular hunt seat sports practiced around the world.

Now let's take a walk on the Western side, and check out what the cowboys are doing.

SECTION 2 : THE WESTERN DISCIPLINES

Some Western riders aim to separate themselves from the cowboy heritage from which the riding style evolved. Others make it a robust lifestyle.

There certainly is something appealing about the imagery of the Wild West. There's a certain amount of do-it-yourself attitude, mixed with utter lawlessness, and the freedom that comes with being 200 miles away from anything. Especially with so many of today's population working in tightly-packed offices and living in close reach of our neighbors in condos and apartment complexes, the vision of watching the sunset from the back of a horse while the cows graze peacefully in the distance is pretty ideal.

You don't need a herd of cattle to enjoy all of the disciplines that fall under the Western umbrella, though. Many of these sports were developed around all of the other practical riding that happens when you're taking care of a farm. You've got the low, flat, and comfortable gaits that were developed for all-day riding. There are activities that test your ability to navigate through expected obstacles as well as those that require you to ride hell-bent for leather like someone's after your hide. As we dig deeper into the Western disciplines, it will become clear that these are sports built out of purpose, though over time, they've become more stylized than what you might expect at the typical working ranch.

One thing that unifies each of the following activities is the saddle. While the English saddle is flat and allows for plenty of hip movement when hunting and racing, the Western saddle is deep with a longer, straighter leg position. This allows for stability and comfort, whether you're riding for a long time or dealing with fast, rapidly changing movements as you might expect when chasing a stray dogie. From this position, an open hip, well-developed core, and soft seat will allow Western riders to remain in place, allowing the horse to do his work.

Western saddles have a distinctive "horn" on the front. This horn comes in various shapes and sizes, depending on its function. It can be used to stabilize a rider while the horse makes lightning-fast adjustments, or you can hang various equipment, such as ropes and saddle bags from it. While Western saddles may look uniform, they can be specifically designed to improve a rider's ability to perform certain jobs— such as the high pommel on a roping saddle. However, a general work saddle will be sufficient for entry-level riding and trying out a few different activities.

Western riding also requires far less contact between the rider's hands and the bit in the horse's mouth than English riding does. In Western riding, the bits are often larger and heavier. The horse is trained to appreciate smaller and softer shifts of the bit. This means the rider can ride on a looser rein. In practical application, this means a rider's hands are more free to open gates, rope cattle, or eat a sandwich, depending on what the day's work brings.

The following chapters will give you an overview of the slow and low, the fast and furious, and all the pattern classes in between that comprise the Western riding disciplines. Take a look and decide for yourself what you and your horse might like to try.

Chapter 1: Pleasure and Patterns

There's something about the balance and effortlessness of the Western jog that I absolutely adore. Legs long and hips open, your seat rocks in an almost imperceivable side to side motion.

Of course, there's way more to it than that. Highly competitive riders know how to accomplish the headset, and the right amount of pause between strides that gives a pleasure horse the most pleasant-appearing gaits. The tiny shifts of balance that happen in the hands to encourage the horse to steer are admirable.

If hunt seat disciplines are divided into "on the flat " and "jumping," then Western disciplines can be divided into Pleasure, Pattern, and Performance. Like hunter classes, Pleasure tends to focus on the horse's performance and appearance. Pattern classes require serious communication between horse and rider, while Performance classes focus on how quickly a horse and rider duo can complete various patterns or tasks. Let's take a look at each.

Western Pleasure

Western pleasure correlates to the hunter on the flat activities that we discussed earlier; the primary difference is the saddle, but there's far more to it than that. While hunt seat riders are encouraged to move forward with open, even, steady gaits, Western riders prefer a slower, more controlled, flat-kneed gait. That's not to say that Western horses *can't* go fast– they are horses, after all– but that they are trained and often bred to produce a range of gaits that are all-day comfortable for both horse and rider.

There are several different activities that traditionally fall under the Western pleasure umbrella. The first is rail work. Rail work is basically what most people do in their lessons or warm up. You walk around the outside of the arena, then jog, lope, switch direction, and do it all again. Sometimes things get exciting, such as multiple changes of direction or walk-to-lope transitions.

Generally speaking, judges in Western pleasure competitions are not looking so much at the rider as the horse. They want to see quality gaits, and an obedient, quiet horse. In breed shows, such as those of the Appaloosa Horse Club, the American Paint Horse Registry, or the American Quarter Horse Association, just to name a few, judges will also focus on how well the horse represents the breed standard.

One question I've heard frequently is, "What is up with the Western pleasure outfits?" Mostly, these words are spoken in awe and fascination. While hunt seat riders are relegated to the muted palette of black, gray, navy, white, and beige, Western pleasure riders are decked out in colorful, bejeweled jackets and brightly colored chaps with long, decadent fringe. Their saddles are slathered with shiny bits of silver, and their coordinated saddle pads are brightly patterned.

This is part of the pageantry that is common in Western shows within the United States. Not all Western disciplines subscribe to this dress code, however. Working classes, such as ranch riding, speed events, reining, and roping, all have a more function-based dress code. Generally, riders in those classes will wear a button down shirt, jeans, chaps, and cowboy boots.

So what's up with the "blinged-out" riders? There are various theories as to where the style originated. Some say it started when horse people from remote farms would meet up in their Sunday best to show off their horses to each other. Others say it's a natural evolution of the suit-style clothing that pleasure riders wore to demonstrate that their horse's gaits were so smooth, they didn't kick up dust.

Most modern riders work for months to create a full custom turnout that will compliment and enhance their horse's appearance. Everything coordinates in a color that contrasts perfectly with the horse's coat. While the horse's coat is polished to an almost mirror-like sheen, the rhinestones in the rider's jacket illuminate their presence with the reflective twinkle of tiny lights.

Watching a high-stakes class like the AQHA Masters can be a festival of lights and colors, making it a truly breathtaking thing to behold. Bear in mind that the pageant is exclusive to the show ring. Much as hunt seat riders rarely wear hunt coats outside of the ring, Pleasure riders school in regular old clothes. In fact, the silver-studded saddles often sit in a place of pride until show weekend arrives. You don't need special equipment to get started with Western pleasure schooling—just a horse.

Horsemanship

Western Horsemanship is, on paper, the opposite of rail work. This class judges a rider's equitation, along with the harmony between horse and rider. Horsemanship is somewhat like dressage, in that horse and rider pairs are asked to perform a series of movements and tasks in order, which challenge their ability to communicate clearly with each other. However, while dressage tests take place in a lettered arena, Horsemanship classes often have cones or other markers to designate where certain movements in the pattern should start and stop. Riders may be asked to ride circles, transition between various gaits, change leads or direction, and back up throughout a horsemanship pattern.

The precision in movements required to complete a Horsemanship pattern accurately is something anyone who works with horses should attempt. Reading the instructions, it doesn't seem too difficult. Take the first three directions of the 2012 AQHA Select World (Finals) Horsemanship as an example:

1. Walk 15 feet
2. Extended jog to middle of arena
3. 360-degree turn to the left followed by 360-degree turn to the right

However, being able to set up for a 360-degree turn right out of a fairly fast jog means knowing exactly where you and your horse's bodies need to be in order to make a seamless, accurate transition. Oh yeah, and the rider's equitation is being judged every step of the way. No pressure!

Horsemanship requires riders to communicate quickly and effectively with their horses. As you'll see from the example tests included in the "Resources" section, each pattern has a different level of difficulty. At the competitive level, you'll likely get a copy of your pattern just a few hours before you enter the ring which adds an extra level of anxiety to the class.

As a result, many Horsemanship riders school as many different patterns as they can find online. The result is clean, careful, and consistent communication between horse and rider, which we should all strive towards, regardless of discipline.

Should you work on these patterns at home, I recommend working on getting the feel for the movements and work involved in executing each movement, then putting them together as a full pattern. Then, only once you and your horse have the idea down, focus on your body position. And don't let frustration win— this is an experience, not an automatic process.

The pattern-based activities continue with Trail, Ranch Riding, and Western Dressage. These terms are sometimes confused with each other or used interchangeably, so it's not uncommon for newer riders to become confused by these three. Let's take a look at each.

Trail

Not to be confused with riding on a trail, Trail classes usually take place in an arena. When riders approach the arena, they will notice a lot of stuff seemingly scattered randomly around almost every inch of the usable ground. Welcome to Trail!

Like Horsemanship, Trail classes challenge horse and rider by requiring them to ride a course. This isn't a jump course, however, though there may be some small cross rails or natural-styled obstacles like logs to hop over. Mostly, these classes test the ability of the horse and rider to communicate successfully while maneuvering over lines of poles, through gates, around poles, and over small platforms known as "bridges." Horse and rider pairs may be asked to walk, trot, lope, or even navigate these obstacles in reverse.

One famous Trail obstacle that I have been asked to practice seemingly millions of times as a young rider, and which I still use today is the "Dog Leg." This obstacle is created by four poles, set parallel to each other, with a 120-degree angle between the two of them. When set up correctly, it will resemble a very open letter "L" or a dog's hind leg. Riders are asked to walk, trot, or lope through the poles, then stop and navigate through the bend in reverse. The goal is to be able to do this with no hesitation of horse or rider, and without stepping on or over the poles.

You don't actually need poles to do this– you can draw lines in the dirt for a very cost-effective version- but you do need a lot of patience. In fact, you might wonder the first few times if it can be done. The secret to success is simply relaxing, thinking ahead, planning carefully, and not over-steering your horse.

This aim for accuracy is the entire point of Trail riding. The idea is to mimic things horse and rider might encounter out on an actual trail, such as opening a gate between fence lines, winding around tightly-planted trees, and stepping over fallen branches or logs in rapid fire succession without losing your footing or concentration.

Many riding instructors feel that schooling these types of obstacles are fantastic for building communication skills and learning how to take one challenge at a time, and I agree. The idea of going over a pole at any gait might seem ridiculously simple, until your horse doesn't pick up his feet and trips over it. While it's unlikely that you or your horse will fall, it will still provide a jarring reminder of how much you rely on each other's balance and coordination. At a trot or lope, going over a line of poles– meaning, several poles in a row with the same number of strides in between them– will require the horse to engage different parts of his body to keep moving in a balanced manner without losing their stride and rhythm. If one of you loses their concentration, it will soon be evident in the clatter of poles.

While you may never desire the Trail class blue ribbon, I highly encourage you to explore some of the Trail obstacles, many of which can be easily created at home. In fact, this is one case where the more rugged materials you use, the more realistic your experience will be!

Ranch Work

Ranch Work essentially takes the concept of Horsemanship, throws a few obstacles into the mix like Trail, and then adds cows. At least, that is how most classes at upper level shows unfold.

Ranch classes are sometimes known as Versatility classes depending on what is being asked of the horse and rider. At some shows, Ranch classes are more of an extreme version of Horsemanship and Trail put together, meaning riders are expected to ride both an equitation-based pattern while going through a course of obstacles. Riders may also be asked to perform "working" gaits, such as the extended jog and extended lope, which ask the horse to take bigger strides with greater impulsion from their hindquarters. It's definitely a sport that requires a lot physically and mentally from horse and rider.

Much as the name implies, Ranch riding mimics what a horse and rider would encounter if they were a working team on a cattle ranch. As a result, some classes involve navigating through and around a pen of cows, though you may or may not have to interact with them. The goal is to demonstrate that the horse has no problem being in the midst of many bovine, and that he remains tuned in to what the rider is asking of him.

So, while all of this is going on in the ring, what are judges looking for? In a nutshell, they're looking for a pair that looks like they'd be right at home on a ranch. Horses are expected to approach each obstacle in stride. They should look comfortable and at ease with no tail swishing or ear pinning. The gaits should be even and the transitions smooth. If a horse stops or refuses to work with an obstacle, it's a penalty.

The great news about Ranch riding is that you can practice at home with very little extra equipment. Some poles will be helpful, and you likely have a gate somewhere that you can practice riding up to, unlatching, walking through, and latching behind you. Many Ranch riding patterns are also available online, which means you can practice the precise transitions, extensions, and turns that are required in competition. You definitely don't ever have to leave home to practice some of the finer points of this riding style.

Western Dressage

Western Dressage has been around as long as people have been sitting in Western saddles, but it has only recently gained recognition as a competitive discipline. I remember watching my first Western Dressage clinic and wondering aloud to a friend whether it was "dressage with a horn." To a certain extent, it truly is.

Many credit trainers Tom and Bill Dorrance with the development of modern Western Dressage. Combining the grace of Classical Dressage and the flexibility and balance required within Horsemanship patterns, the goal of the sport is to encourage lightness, forward motion, and balance. The Dorrance brothers initially formulated dressage-based training techniques as a way to create a mental and physical bond between horses of any breed and riders of all backgrounds that could result in a long, healthy relationship and working career.

And then it took off! Western Dressage is now recognized by the American Quarter Horse Association (AQHA) and the United States Equestrian Federation (USEF). Trainers across the country are specializing in Western Dressage, making the sport increasingly available for riders everywhere.

Much as in classical dressage, Western Dressage horse and rider teams are asked to ride a test composed of several different movements that demonstrate forward, fluid working gaits. Conceptually, based on movements that a working Ranch horse might need to execute when working, the tests range from Intro to Level 5. Horse and rider duos may be asked to walk, jog, lope, and demonstrate collection and extension in those gaits. Pivots, pirouettes, half-passes, circles, and serpentines are added to illustrate the team's suppleness and harmony.

Western Dressage is something every horse and rider can benefit from, as its principles require keen communication between you and your beast. Practicing skills that require balance, flexibility, and forwardness can help you find solutions for big challenges, regardless of what disciplines you normally ride. And while Western Dressage tests generally take place in a lettered arena, just like hunt seat dressage, you really don't need anything to start trying out some of the test movements on your own. Practice forward, collaborative gaits, straight lines, and circles, or download one of the online tests provided by the Western Dressage Association of America (WDAA). Don't focus on making the ride look perfect—focus on having the best possible ride for you and your horse.

Pleasure and Pattern riding is the bread and butter of the Western disciplines. The Performance sports—which we'll look at next—require riders to be steady and capable in both Pleasure and Pattern riding in order to pull off the athletic demands of each sport. While these disciplines may not seem as high-adrenaline as speed events, they are challenging, as horse and rider are constantly asked to challenge their skills and ability each stride of the way.

Chapter 2 : High Performance Western Sports

The title of this chapter is not to imply that there isn't a high level of performance and passion involved with other Western disciplines but that these particular sports add the elements of speed and agility to the skills built upon in Pleasure and Pattern type classes.

Though we're barely scraping the surface of what's involved in each discipline, I hope the following descriptions help get you as amped up about reining and speed events as the competitors themselves. These classes are always a big draw at large shows thanks to the fast-paced, adrenaline-soaked thrills of each competitor's round. Will this horse be faster? Slide further? Or will this horse hit a barrel on their way through the turns? The sense of danger is great, as a single misstep at these high speeds could lead to a major spill.

One of the most admirable qualities of high performance Western sports is the finely tuned communication between horse and rider. Reining horses are trained to perform a pattern in a manner that appears effortless. Contesting horses may seem like fire-breathing locomotives out of the ring, but once the gate opens, they're all business, finding the swiftest place to put each hoof in rapid succession. The rider, meanwhile, urges on their horse in levels of excitement ranging from subtle and synchronistic to so enthusiastic that the pair seems to leave common physics behind as they hover above the ground in pursuit of the fastest time.

Much as show jumping and cross country are considered some of the more high-performance sports performed in an English saddle, reining and contesting would hold similar positions in Western riding, though the purpose and nuances of each sport are different. Read on to determine if you and your horse are able–

or even willing– to pursue these performanced-based Western sports.

Reining

Technically speaking, reining is a pattern-based discipline. However, since the

whole pattern is performed at a lope or gallop, this is definitely a high performance

element. And when you factor in an arena full of eager spectators whooping and

whistling as the horse and rider perform moves like rollbacks, sliding stops, and

spins, the adrenaline really starts pumping.

At the basis of every reining pattern is the demonstration of being able to ride a

smooth, forward circle of various sizes and at different speeds, as well as being able

to gallop in straight lines, ending with the physics-defying, seemingly zero-friction,

sliding stop. Add into the mix the horse making rapid spins while planted on a single

hind hoof, all seemingly without a single cue or request from the rider. According to

the National Reining Horse Association (NRHA):

"To rein a horse is not only to guide him, but also to control his every movement.

The best reined horse should be willingly guided or controlled with little or no

apparent resistance and dictated to completely... credit should be given for

smoothness, finesse, attitude, quickness and authority of performing various

maneuvers, while using controlled speed."

- *2017 NHRA Pattern Guide (https://nrha.com/media/pdf/2017/patterns.pdf)*

    Page 4

Of course, appearances can be deceiving. Riding a correct reining pattern requires

intense concentration on behalf of both horse and rider. Having had the pleasure

to work with top-notch professional reiners, I admire their enthusiasm and determination for performing well. The riders are extremely dedicated to their sport, too!

Practicing intermittent slow and fast, large and small circles at every gait is a great exercise for every horse and rider team;. However, I will caution against attempting fast spins or sliding stops without a special hind shoe called a "sliding shoe" or "slider". This type of shoe has a shiny, flat metal surface that allows the horse to glide on arena footing, while their natural hooves provide a certain amount of built-in grip. A horse without sliders can still perform these moves, but he won't be able to replicate the twenty-foot slides you see at the professional level, and it will create a certain amount of wear and tear to his hindlimb joints.

To add a little bit of reining to your training, try seeing how much you can accomplish with the smallest possible cues. This will take lots of practice, but you'll start to discover how clenching the reins, twisting your wrist, or shifting your weight forward or back in the saddle can impact how your horse moves. These principles are what make a reiner look so graceful and at ease and translate well into success in other disciplines as well.

Speed Events

I'd like to start this overview of timed equine events with a confession: I'm not aware of every single mounted speed event. I know of the major ones such as Barrel Racing, Pole Bending, and Mounted Shooting. But then we get into the somewhat uncivilized world of the local Gymkhana and its mix of familiar mounted games and regional competitions that likely evolved from a dare. Nearly every long-time horse person has looked at a show bill in another county or state, pointed at a speed event class name, and asked, "What's that class about?"

While some speed events are sanctioned with distinct rules and regulations, others declare their winner by who arrives at the finish line in one piece the fastest. For some riders, this can sound like terrifying territory. For others, it's the best thing in the whole wide world.

I don't like to generalize, but there are certain people who are confirmed thrill seekers. Some people enjoy skydiving and bungee jumping. Some seek out the tallest, fastest, and scariest roller coasters. Others compete in speed-based riding events. There may be overlap between these groups, as well.

If pattern work is all about precision, speed events only amplify that particular talent. Depending on the size of the arena, a barrel course can be over in anywhere between fifteen and thirty seconds. Allow me to emphasize the word *seconds*. By the time you have finished reading this sentence word for word, a barrel racer will have galloped into the arena, raced at top speed around three barrels in a cloverleaf pattern– which includes at least one lead change– and dashed out of the arena while the crowd loudly cheers them on.

Some speed events are clearly designed as races. Down and Back is an activity that only involves one turn, though the horse and rider are instead responsible for sprinting from the in-gate to the end of the arena, swiftly spin around a single barrel, and practically teleport themselves back to the in-gate at top speed.

Other timed events involve more complicated tasks. Mounted Shooting, for example, requires horse and rider to dash through an arena, riding a pattern while aiming two .45 caliber single action revolvers at up to ten balloons tied to poles. The goal is to shoot as many balloons as possible without having to circle back.

Another fun feature of Mounted Shooting is that the official sport organization, the Cowboy Mounted Shooting Association (CMSA) encourages members to turn back time and dress in attire that wouldn't be out of place in a cowboy movie. Much as field hunting captures the pageantry of Olde England, Mounted Shooting invokes the spirit of the Wild West with collarless shirts, button jeans, and weathered cowboy hats.

If the idea of trying a variety of mounted speed events and conquering many different obstacles while the clock ticks away amuses you, you might seek out a Gymkhana. The definition of Gymkhana is generally accepted to be, "...a variety of mounted speed events and timed obstacles courses," because the classes you might encounter at one can be so varied. In the equestrian world, we joke that Gymkhana is pure lawless thrills, but there are certainly rules to each competition in addition to having the fastest possible time.

You might encounter some of the speed classes previously mentioned at a Gymkhana event, along with some other fascinating races. For example, you and a partner might be asked to race through cones while each holding the opposite end of a swatch of toilet paper. Riders may be asked to balance an egg on a spoon while weaving through poles or completing a pattern based on Horsemanship skills. Back when phone books were large, impressive tomes, riders would race each other to a phone book placed in the far end of an arena with the goal of being the first to tear out a specific page and hustle back to the starting line. These might seem like silly races to have, but they are a true test of one's ability to ride accurately and athletically.

It is almost unheard of in the equestrian community for a rider to not be challenged to a race of some sort by another rider, especially if you happen to keep your horse at a boarding barn with similarly aged and skilled equestrians. I have many happy memories of "pole bending" with my first horse as we wove through a line of jump standards we dragged out from the side of the arena. My large Thoroughbred was only able to trot the maneuvers, because of how tall, long, and gangly he was, while a girl with a small sway-backed pony of undetermined breeding left us in the dust. When it comes to being quick, knowing your center of gravity and the boundaries of what you and your horse can do are often just as important— if not more— than being big and trained to go fast.

One word of caution, however— speed events really can be dangerous, as horses can lose their balance and crash to the ground. I strongly encourage anyone who wants to try these events to get comfortable at all gaits first, then start with trying the patterns at a low speed before going full-out at a dead gallop. You'll note that the organizations associated with these sports have different requirements for riders ranging from beginner to highly experienced, so while it's good to challenge yourself, don't overface yourself. And don't be afraid to wear a helmet!

With Bovine Assistance

The term "cowboy" implies that there are cows somehow involved in Western riding, but so far, we have seen very few actual horned, hooved, milk-producing ruminants. With the exception of the potential for a pen of cattle in Ranch Work, all of these events involve a horse and rider pair.

There's Cutting, Roping, Team Roping, Team Penning, Cattle Working, Ranch Sorting, Reined Cow Horse, and more... It may be difficult for a brand new cowboy to decide where they should put their focus. Each class is a bit different, but success at home, on the range, and in the ring hinges on one very important factor:

Your horse has to be okay with cows.

Technically speaking, any breed can participate in cattle events, from the flashy Andalusian horses that appear at the end of a bullfight to the rough-and-ready American stock horse. However, your horse's breeding is completely irrelevant if the poor thing can't tolerate cattle.

You would think that horses and cattle would get along, in a similarly minded, herd-oriented prey animal sort of way. But cows smell funny, and they make weird noises, and there are some horses that will refuse to share their space with them for any significant amount of time. I had one horse who, despite boldly jumping over giant cross country courses and the fence line of his pasture to go exploring, would spook so significantly at the mere whiff of a nearby cow that his soul would appear to leave his body. Some horses are just not interested in interspecies activities.

However, if you are blessed with a horse that enjoys playing with other farm animals, cattle events are always a treat. Regardless of the particular sport practiced under this broad term, riding with cows requires horse and rider to work together to outwit the cow and control it's actions.

Penning, for example, involves separating several cows from the herd and moving them into a separate pen without losing control of the herd. Sorting involves finding specifically numbered cattle in a herd and working them into isolation away from the herd. Cow Working is similar to using your horse to guide a cow through a Horsemanship pattern. Roping– as the name suggests– involves horse and rider chasing a calf and snaring it in a lariat, requiring speed, agility, precision, and impressive wrist action.

It's unfair to relegate a group of sports to a brief series of sentences, especially when cow horses represent a very important part of American heritage. In fact, horses are still an important part of working ranch life, even today.

Still, not everyone has the opportunity to try cattle events because of the specific requirements involved; specifically, the cattle portion. If you are interested in working cattle, you might need to search a little harder for a trainer and opportunities to learn, depending on your location. Of course, you could substitute goats, as they do at many rodeos, but then you have to get the goat to agree to your shenanigans!

Western Roundup

Western riding is popular not only for the comfortable saddles and the glitz of the show pen but for all of the opportunities to ride a diverse number of different disciplines and styles. Though there may be overlap in some instances such as the intense variety of pattern-based classes, each Western sport has been designed to test the mental and physical athleticism of both horse and rider.

The difference in dynamic between Western riding versus English is truly fascinating. Both were born out of tradition and necessity. Western disciplines celebrate the working tradition of the ranch, while English disciplines are based on hunting across the wild countryside and military movements. Still, the overall principles are the same: accuracy, collaboration, and a true sense of communication between horse and rider.

Now let's take a look at some of the sports that don't fall specifically under "English" or "Western" riding but that still provide plenty of opportunity for engagement and development between you and your horse.

SECTION 3 : FUN FOR EVERYONE

I would like to start this section with an apology: for those who ride the following disciplines, I am sorry they haven't received as large a chunk of the book as the English and Western sports.

I appreciate all equestrian sports equally, and I think it's a shame when you've trained your entire life, only to be relegated to a short sentence or footnote in a book about horses. Realistically, each activity and subsection of this book deserves its own book in order to fully reveal and discuss the complexities and rewards of participating in that particular sport. However, my task has been to provide a brief overview to pique your interest or help you decide you're definitely not getting involved with a sport that doesn't fit you and your horse's goals very well.

I started with English and Western disciplines because they are prevalent in training barns across the United States. If you conduct an online search for "riding stable near me," you'll likely see descriptions that lead with "Western riding style," or "focus on hunter jumper training." I want to set you up with the information you'll need to navigate these descriptions as well as find your footing for progressing through the discipline you'd like to explore further.

So what are the sports that don't fit the English/Western dichotomy? Are they rogue outliers representing some type of equine anarchy? Not quite. Every type of equestrian interaction is descended from long-running tradition based on the very reasons we domesticated horses in the first place. Though we do not rely on horses for work purposes as much as we once did, we're still inexplicably drawn to the sports and activities that bring us closer to these majestic animals; Therefore, I would like to apologize to anyone who's equestrian sport of choice is not adequately represented here.

Though I have merely skimmed over a few disciplines, I have included reference material in the "Resources" section about as many opportunities for equine interaction as I could find. Look for these under the "Other Sports and Activities" section.

There are a few specific disciplines that I'd like to highlight, as I believe they are fundamental and available to a wide variety of equestrians around the world, including enjoying your gaited horse, riding out of the ring on trails, driving, and taking part in in-hand sports. Take a look to see if you and your horse might enjoy some of these options.

Saddleseat and Gaited Horses

I would love to get into the differences between the various Gaited Horse and Saddleseat disciplines and how Western pleasure has different rules and expectations when at a sponsored breed show, such as the American Morgan Horse Association (AMHA) or the Arabian Horse Association (AHA). I could spend pages regaling new equestrians about the finer points of the five-gaited Saddlebred versus the three-gaited Saddlebred.

However, these disciplines require very specific horses. The term "gaited horse" describes any equine who naturally performs gaits beyond the recognized walk, trot/jog, or canter/lope. Standardbreds may possess the ability to pace or move in such a way that both legs on each side of the body move at once, creating a lateral gait similar to the trot. Paso Fino horses have a variety of gaits that involve rapid footfalls but very little forward movement. Saddlebreds, Tennessee Walkers, Missouri Fox Trotters, and Icelandic, Hackey, and Rocky Mountain horses are just a few examples of gaited horses commonly found in the United States. Unfortunately, these gaits are innate, meaning they come from years of keen breeding. You can't really train a Thoroughbred or a Quarter Horse to perform these gaits.

There is no universal way to ride a gaited horse. The rider's attire and tack used varies depending on the type of activity being performed. Many gaited horse shows include classes that sound familiar such as Horsemanship, dressage, or hunt seat equitation. However, the structure of the class has been updated to showcase the horse's unique gaits, which are not usually demonstrated in non-gaited versions of these activities.

It's also important to note that gaited horses can do far more than gait around in circles. Gaited horses can be ridden in an English or Western saddle, or no saddle at all! I've met several gaited horses who have competed successfully in non-breed specific events, such as three day eventing, western dressage, and trail.

You may wish to work with a trainer who specializes in gaited horses; however, keep in mind that you have the freedom to do whatever you want with your horse as long as it's safe and makes both of you happy!

Perhaps riding your horse in a ring or arena isn't possible or even desirable. Maybe you and your horse were designed to explore the trails less taken.

There are a variety of activities that require nothing more than a trail or an open area to explore. Endurance, Trail Riding, and Competitive Trail Riding are just a few of the equine sports that test the horse and rider's ability to not only function out in the open, but excel and thrive.

Endurance is not just the name of an equine sport— it's the main quality both horse and rider need to display to practice or compete successfully. These races take place over courses of fifty to one hundred mile distances, though limited distance rides of twenty-five to thirty-five miles are offered. This means navigating your horse over variable terrain for an entire day and pausing at regulated intervals for rest holds, during which the horse's vital signs are taken to ensure the long hike isn't having an adverse effect on him.

"The World's Best Known and Most Difficult Equestrian Endurance Ride" is the Tevis Cup, according to their promotional material. Hosted by the Western States Trail Foundation since 1955, this endurance ride covers one hundred miles of ground in just one day, including a hike up Cougar Rock, which is famous for requiring a near-vertical climb.

Of course, not every Endurance competition is held in the Rocky Mountains. Many are hosted on flat land, and riders are asked to navigate a series of loops through a small trail system. These trails are usually marked, but riders are encouraged to take a map and know basic orientation just in case a trail marker wanders off in the wind or weather.

If riding out on the trails in a competitive manner sounds like a good time, but you're not sure you have a full day of equine mountain climbing in you, perhaps Competitive Trail Riding is more your speed— literally.

Competitive Trail Riding, or CTR, is specifically not a race and is open to all riders above age 10, and horses of all breeds. Riders are expected to pace themselves through the course, generally moving no faster than 6 miles per hour. Several veterinary checks are performed throughout the ride and awards are given to the horse who is in the best overall condition once the ride has concluded.

While on the trail, the goal of CTR is to navigate the mapped course while performing certain judged tasks or obstacles, such as mounting your horse from the surrounding terrain, climbing up and down hills, stepping over logs or through water crossings, and backing up at a judge's request. It's important to remember you are not in a hurry; therefore, you can take your time setting up for each of these tasks.

Though CTR is a judged event, it is designed as more of a social activity for equestrians, much like field hunting. Riders are encouraged to help each other out and keep an eye on each other while they're out on the course, and local and regional CTR group members are often fantastic friends in addition to being fierce competitors.

However, you may not want the added pressure of being judged while you trail ride your horse. Great news: You are absolutely encouraged to ride your horse on the trails with friends and family. Riding alone on the trails is not recommended for novice riders simply due to the increased risk of the unknown on the trails. Despite the slow pace of a trail ride, you still need to have a stable seat, functional equitation, and clear communication between horse and rider.

If you do decide to ride alone, wear thick boots, pants, and a helmet, and take plenty of water and your phone with you in case of emergency. Your horse may be a really swell guy, but there are situations you may encounter on the trail that you might not have considered before. For example, during Red's first trail ride, a branch that had been broken in a recent wind storm jarred loose and dropped directly on his head. He spooked and spun around to gallop back to the trailer, dumping my trainer in the process. That's a fair reaction to the situation, but had his stablemates not been there to convince him to stay, my trainer may have had a long and painful walk through the woods in an attempt to locate my horse. Danger is quite literally everywhere on the trails, which is why some people gravitate towards the relative perceived safety of the arena.

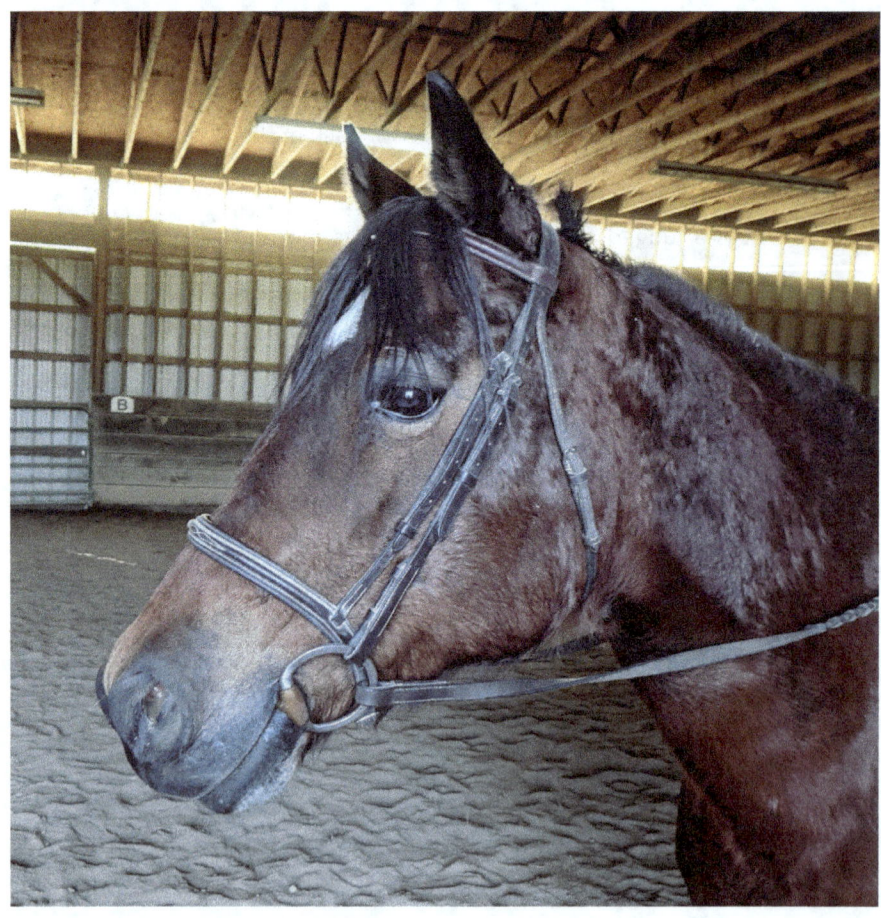

That being said, I truly hope each and every person reading this book has the experience of seeing the world between a horse's ears someday. I've had the pleasure of riding in national parks across the American West, including a memorable ride through the Tetons on a horse that had just arrived in Wyoming two days before. It might be more fair to call that an endurance ride, though, because we were traveling awfully fast for most of it!

If you'd like to test the strength of your communication skills with your horse, I strongly recommend finding your way out to a trail system. Make sure the trails are approved for equine use before you trailer out to the site, and be sure to pack plenty of water for both you and your horse. Who knows— this little ride through the woods might spark a lifelong passion for exploring!

A Different View Between the Horse's Ears

How about driving? While driving a horse remains one of my "bucket list" goals, the various things horses can do in harness is absolutely fascinating. When you ride a horse, you communicate with your hands, arms, shoulders, back, seat, and legs. When you drive a horse, you communicate through reins, a whip, and your voice.

Like trail riding, any breed of horse can participate in Carriage Driving sports. Miniature horses are extremely popular in the driving world, as they're perfectly sized to cart around a novice driver of nearly any age.

Just like the mounted sports, the athletic requirements of Carriage Driving depend on the sport practiced. Nearly everything a rider can do can be accomplished as a driver. Pleasure Driving, much like Horsemanship, involves navigating the horse through a course of maneuvers— in this case marked with cones topped with balls. While making turns, going forward, and backing up, a fault is incurred when a ball topples off of its cone.

Combined Driving is parallel to Three Day Eventing, as riders compete in three separate tests: Dressage, Marathon, and Obstacle Driving. Dressage includes a test comprised of movements that largely mirror that of classical and Western Dressage. The Marathon phase requires teams to navigate a cross country obstacle course that involves completing hills, water crossings, and a labyrinth in the quickest time. Obstacle Driving asks teams to pass through up to twenty "gates," which are pairs of cones and balls set up so drivers must guide the horse and carriage through them swiftly and without disturbing the balls, much as a stadium jump course asks riders not to knock the poles off of the fences they jump.

There are also many arena driving classes, in which pairs of horse and rider drive along the rail to impress the judges with their spectacular turnout, expressive horse, and overall compliance with the image of a cheerful carriage ride on a sunny day.

When putting your horse in harness, I strongly recommend a trainer who has started horses in the lines before, especially if your equine companion has never done this. Some horses protest to things being behind their hindquarters, while others are unfamiliar with the feeling of something dragging behind them. From there, however, the world of driven events opens up, with options like skijoring in the snow or taking friends and family for pony cart rides on the front lawn.

You Don't Have to Ride

I've mentioned this several times throughout this book, but it bears mentioning on its own:

You don't have to ride to enjoy your horse.

There are many activities that allow you to participate with your horse in-hand, or on a lead rope, instead of in the saddle or behind the harness. The groundwork we discussed in the first part of this book can be the start and end point for your work with your horse.

At shows, you can find in-hand classes. Halter and Showmanship allow horse and human combinations to show off conformation and communication equally as the handler asks the horse to perform various movements at the request of the judge. There may be a pattern to work as well, generally consisting only of walk and trot movements, with some halted pivots or turns and backing up a few steps.

To add a little zest to the equation, in-hand trail classes ask riders to perform over, around, and through many of the obstacles found in a Mounted Trail class. It's not a simple matter of having your horse follow you around the arena, though. Horses are expected to travel with their left shoulder aligned with the handler's right shoulder regardless of which in-hand class they choose, which means sharing the same space. As a result, the handlers and horses must have the ability to communicate clearly with each other to avoid collisions over poles or squeezing through gates.

While commonly associated with younger horses, every equestrian should try out the concepts of in-hand trail, especially when in the introductory stage of getting to know your horse. You can use basic PVC poles or even pool noodles to create low-cost obstacles and use one of the online patterns as your guide. Mounted Trail patterns can also be adapted to in-hand trail use by eliminating the lope.

There are so many things to do with horses that I hope to eventually write a book to dig deeper into each activity. However, I hope this brief overview has provided you with enough inspiration to encourage you to check out a few new things to try with your horse.

Even if you don't pursue any of these activities professionally, applying the basics to your next work session can really make a difference in your ability to communicate with your horse. You may not want to switch things up until you and your horse have really hit your stride— literally and figuratively— though remember, there's no shame in starting at the very beginning and working your way towards the more advanced levels with practice.

In fact, starting with a basic, "Hello," and building towards your short and long-term goals is exactly the type of relationship I would recommend you establish with your horse. I also encourage you to let the process take as long as it needs for both you and your horse to feel completely comfortable forging forward.

CONCLUSION

In conclusion, respect your horse. Spend time with him. Learn how to talk not just at him, but with him. Find things the two of you can do together that you both enjoy, and appreciate each and every moment you have together... even if you sometimes wish your horse could spend the night at Grandma's house when he acts up.

When I say, "Love your horse," I don't necessarily mean hugging, kissing, and professing your undying affection for him every single day, though by all means, feel free to do just that. Instead, I encourage you to build an affectionate bond with him. Earlier, I referred to this as a "good working relationship," and that's exactly what you should strive towards.

Consider your horse as you would your coworkers. At your jobsite, you may find colleagues with whom you have an instant bond. You have similar interests or sensibilities, and you love hanging out beyond the workplace. There is also that special breed of coworker with whom you don't mind having a meal or happy hour celebration with, but you probably wouldn't invite them to your wedding. Then, you have the coworkers with whom you are able to accomplish great things in the office, but it would never occur to you to invite them to lunch.

Many people believe that they must have the type of bond with their horse that makes them super besties no matter what they're doing. In all reality, not all horse-human bonds work out that way. That doesn't mean you've failed. In my own life, I've had the privilege of working with a full kaleidoscope of equine personalities. I've had horses who love to snuggle, and I've had horses who were almost offended when I patted them with affection. The physical and emotional aspects of the relationship aren't measured in the same way as what the two of you can accomplish together.

That being said, one of your goals may be to find your heart horse. The term "heart horse" has been coined to describe a horse who is you in horse form. The legend goes that every equestrian has at least one heart horse, with whom they bond instantly and on an entirely different level than any other horse. From experience, I can tell you that this is a real phenomenon. From the moment I slipped a halter on Red's skinny face, I knew that we were already on the same page. Communicating with your heart horse is almost instantaneous; cooperation is a different story, however.

Earlier, we talked about what to do if your horse doesn't like you. I explained that horses generally don't dislike people without reason. Now that you've read this book, I suggest that you reframe the concept. It's likely not *you* that the horse doesn't like, so much as what you're *doing.* That can range from dislike of the brush you're using at a particular moment, to a general distaste for the discipline you're currently schooling. If your horse is communicating to you that he's cranky, bored, or uncomfortable, try something else.

And now you have a whole range of "something elses" to try. The second section of this book focused on the various things that can be done with horses, and as I've admitted, I barely managed to skim the first layer of detail. Equestrian sports are some of the oldest athletic activities on this planet. Born from human need, each sport has developed into a test of a horse and handler's ability to communicate and accomplish great things together. I encourage everyone to check out the "Resources" section at the end of this book to help you and your horse safely and correctly navigate the waters that come with learning about a new horse. I strongly recommend at least learning the fundamentals from a professional in the discipline that intrigues you so that you're aware of how to safely and correctly practice your chosen activity for a long time.

You don't need to ever walk in the show ring to be successful at these disciplines, either. You may choose to go to fun shows, where the only requirement is a helmet and boots, or aim for events that cost money and earn you points on the circuit. The gauge of success isn't ribbons, trophies, or medals, but in how much enjoyment you and your horse get from your activities. Yes, it's very nice to have a physical manifestation of your ability to cooperate with a 1,000-pound prey animal, but the real accomplishment is the cooperation itself. At the end of the day, a ribbon is just a bit of fabric, and a trophy is just some metal. Points are arbitrary and usually expire at the end of a season. The thrill and serenity that comes from that working relationship with a horse, however? That lasts a lifetime.

Enjoy your horse, and tell him I send my regards!

RESOURCES

The internet has a seemingly infinite amount of information about absolutely anything horse-related. It should go without saying that not all of this information is of the same quality or accuracy. Additionally, different trainers will have different perspectives on what success looks like, as their formula for training has been carefully developed through their own experiences. That is to say, every trainer is going to feel that their recipe for winning is the "correct" method.

Therefore, I've done my best to collect unbiased resources that can provide you with further information on the topics discussed in this book. Please don't consider these endorsements of any kind, but rather a gathering of launch pads from which you can find your own rabbit hole. I've tried to include official websites wherever possible to ensure that you're starting with the official word on each matter.

I'm not personally affiliated with any breed or sport organization, either. Belle is registered with AQHA, but as I don't intend to show or breed her, that's mainly to establish and maintain my rights as her legal owner. Red is registered through the Jockey Club, and though his registry rights were never transferred to me, his purchase was documented through an agent for his previous owner.

As you read these, please don't consider them a personal endorsement, as I get no kickback or benefit from these sites or links. Instead, understand that I considered these very thorough and comprehensive guides to help you get settled on the path to happiness with your equine companion.

Enjoy!

Bonding and Communication Work

The following links lead to groundwork and communication exercises for horse and human. Though I mention these exercises in the context of introducing yourself to your horse, remember that you can step back and refresh your communication skills with your horse at any time.

As I mentioned, each expert has a different methodology, so I've attempted to bring you a variety of perspectives in the following sites:

Monty Roberts : https://montyroberts.com/

Clinton Anderson: https://downunderhorsemanship.com/

Warwick Schiller: https://www.warwickschiller.com/

Craig Cameron: https://craigcameron.com/

Jim Thomas: http://barthorsemanship.com/

Exercises:

https://equinehelper.com/5-best-groundwork-exercises-for-your-horse/

https://www.youtube.com/watch?v=YZFjsf5t0cM

https://www.youtube.com/watch?v=n0kVp4oU8Q8

English Riding

The following sites and videos will help provide a visual to complement what you've just read, in addition to providing you with your first stepping stone through the doorway of hunt seat riding sports.

Riding on the Flat

Lynn Palm: http://www.lynnpalm.com/

Note: Ms. Palm is also a fantastic resource on the matter of Western Dressage, should you find interest in that topic, as well.

USEF: https://www.usef.org/compete/disciplines/hunter-seat-equitation

US Pony Club: https://www.ponyclub.org/Members/Disciplines/HunterSeatEquitation/

Videos:

https://www.youtube.com/watch?v=atvDIXPTmKg

https://www.youtube.com/watch?v=oxWHHigKW1E

Show Jumping

USEF: https://www.usef.org/compete/disciplines/jumping

Understanding Courses: https://www.horsejournals.com/riding-training/english/hunter-jumper/how-walk-jump-course

US Pony Club: https://www.ponyclub.org/members/disciplines/showjumping/

Videos:

https://www.youtube.com/watch?v=eT1WygNY0n8

https://www.youtube.com/watch?v=d4PyKUqR96Q

Cross Country / Three Day Eventing

USEF: https://www.usef.org/compete/disciplines/eventing

Dressage: https://useventing.com/events-competitions/resources/dressage-tests

Cross Country:https://horseandcountry.tv/en-us/cross-country-horse-riding-for-beginners/

Stadium: https://useventing.com/resources/documents/The-Basics-of-Jumping-Course-Design-for-Eventing.pdf

Videos:

"The Event Formerly known as Rolex" is one of the top Three-Day Events in the world. Currently known as the Land Rover Kentucky Three Day Event, you can see some of the top riders in the sport on this course:

https://www.youtube.com/watch?v=TnL26YXBwt8

https://www.youtube.com/watch?v=sNRt6Od6COo

https://www.youtube.com/watch?v=DCrL580E7Zk

https://www.youtube.com/watch?v=Yc-UGH6ms5U

Field Hunting

Is Your Horse Ready?, by Old North Bridge Hounds: https://oldnorthbridge-hounds.org/2009/11/17/is-your-horse-ready-to-hunt/

MFHA: https://mfha.com/

A History in North America, from Fox Hunting Life: https://www.foxhuntinglife.com/american-foxhunting

Sidesaddle: http://www.americansidesaddleassociation.org/

Videos:

https://www.youtube.com/watch?v=-1HyfOYjJZk

https://www.youtube.com/watch?v=FXtrv11h8tE

Western Riding

The following links will help you learn more about the low and slow, precise and nice, and adrenaline-soaked versions of the style that was developed by working riders on the range.

Overview

Types of Riding: https://horserookie.com/what-are-different-types-western-riding/

Pleasure

AQHA: https://www.aqha.com/western-pleasure

A History: http://www.parksonline.org/equestrians/sports/western01.html

The Basics: https://www.horsejournals.com/riding-training/western/western-pleasure/basics-showing-western-pleasure

Videos:

https://www.youtube.com/watch?v=Bb7kN6jaKps

https://www.youtube.com/watch?v=vRywYlwIIEk

Horsemanship

Patterns: https://www.aqha.com/-/13-aqha-horsemanship-patterns-for-you-to-practice

How To: https://www.horseillustrated.com/horse-exclusives-horsemanship-pattern

AQHA: https://www.aqha.com/-/horse-showing-in-a-pattern-class

Videos:

https://www.youtube.com/watch?v=PwGi8m1gHvo

Equal parts informative and video: https://horses.extension.org/judging-horse-events-western-horsemanship/

Trail

Trail Obstacles: https://trailriderchallenge.com/trc-explained/obstacles/

AQHA: https://www.aqha.com/trail

Trail Patterns: http://www.showhorsepromotions.com/trailpatterns.htm

Videos:

https://www.youtube.com/watch?v=tYnQpa5TN1g

https://www.youtube.com/watch?v=OPVSkSt5c6g&t=188s

Ranch Riding

AQHA: https://www.aqha.com/ranch-riding1

Patterns: https://www.aqha.com/aqha-show-patterns

Please note- this link includes direction to all AQHA patterns, including other disciplines and sports. You can explore them all from the menu.

How To: https://www.farnam.com/stable-talk/maximize-your-scores-in-ranch-riding

Videos:

https://www.youtube.com/watch?v=Z8p4ybBsFY8

https://www.youtube.com/watch?v=26TyQ9lcXIg

Western Dressage

WDAA: https://www.westerndressageassociation.org/

Western Dressage Tests: https://wdaa.memberclicks.net/wdaa-tests

USEF: https://www.usef.org/compete/disciplines/western-dressage

Videos:

https://www.youtube.com/watch?v=ClHuAg9RNOw

https://www.youtube.com/watch?v=xe4-LlKHN2w

Reining

NRHA Patterns: https://nrha.com/media/pdf/2017/patterns.pdf

FEI: https://www.fei.org/stories/sport/reining/everything-you-need-know-about-reining

AQHA: https://www.aqha.com/-/seven-tips-for-stepping-up-your-reining-game

Videos:

https://www.youtube.com/watch?v=cqbYdyTbODE

https://www.youtube.com/watch?v=4YCgsZmjsww

Speed Events

Kristin Weaver Brown: http://kristinweaverbrown.com/

NBHA: https://nbha.com/

Gymkhana: https://timetoride.org/riders/about-horses/horse-activities/contesting-gymkhana/

Gymkhana Games: https://horseyhooves.com/mounted-horse-games/

Videos:

https://www.youtube.com/watch?v=n0Qk5tsJz4o

https://www.youtube.com/watch?v=ibvovCudG_s

Cowboy Mounted Shooting

CMSA: https://www.cmsaevents.com/about/

AQHA: https://www.aqha.com/-/give-it-a-shot-part-1

Videos:

https://www.youtube.com/watch?v=XBsr4aT7tmA

https://www.youtube.com/watch?v=YO5B8zR7F3c

Cattle Events

Cattle Events Explained: https://www.horseillustrated.com/category/riding-and-training/disciplines/cattle-events

Reined Cow Horse: https://nrcha.com/affiliate-events/

Working Cow Horse: https://www.aqha.com/working-cow-horse

Cutting: https://nchacutting.com/

Roping: https://equinewellnessmagazine.com/horse-roping/

Videos:

https://www.youtube.com/watch?v=6g4f9gxGO9Y

https://www.youtube.com/watch?v=nUZ2gxcBHBo

Other Sports and Activities

Saddle Seat

Understanding the Sport: https://www.horseillustrated.com/horse-exclusives-saddleseat-judge-myths

USEF: https://www.usef.org/compete/disciplines/saddle-seat/usa-saddle-seat

US Saddle Seat: https://www.ussaddleseat.com/

Videos:

https://www.youtube.com/watch?v=15cHhqvevT4

https://www.youtube.com/watch?v=X_7z8pvqXPc

Endurance

AERC: https://www.aerc.org/

FEI: https://www.fei.org/endurance

Tevis Cup: http://www.teviscup.org/

Videos:

https://www.youtube.com/watch?v=MWsi1Uc_MbA

https://www.youtube.com/watch?v=s2J-3j8ueoo

Trail Riding and Competitive Trail Riding

NATRC: https://www.natrc.org/

Trail Riding Safety: https://horseandrider.com/trail-riding/trail-riding-safety-tips-15710

How To: https://equusmagazine.com/riding/build-trustworthy-trail-horse-10655/

Videos:

https://www.youtube.com/watch?v=Ti5wfyD_kIo

https://www.youtube.com/watch?v=pVP3xwkeS2M

Driving

World Horse Driving Association: https://www.worldhorsedriving.com/com-petition-info#:~:text=September%202021-,About%20the%20sport,dres-sage%2C%20marathon%20and%20obstacle%20driving.

General Driving Information: http://www.theshowring.info/Driving.htm

US Equestrian Carriage Driving Guide: https://www.usequestrian.org/compete/resources-forms/disciplines/carriage-pleasure-driving

https://www.americandrivingsociety.org/content.aspx?page_id=22&club_id=548049&module_id=407752

Videos:

https://www.youtube.com/watch?v=owwwmdc6S-M

https://www.youtube.com/watch?v=eNKOsd-zKd4

Halter and In-Hand

Halter:

https://www.horseillustrated.com/horse-showing-how-to-show-in-halter-classes

Showmanship: https://www.horseillustrated.com/western-horse-training-showmanship-dos-and-donts

In-Hand Trail:

https://passionatehorsemanship.com/8499/difference-between-horse-agility-and-in-hand-trail-or-halter-obstacle/

Videos:

https://www.youtube.com/watch?v=NrvU0YcdtEU

https://www.youtube.com/watch?v=l8bcetss8SM

Polo

Though not mentioned in the main text, Polo is a thrilling sport in which horse and rider chase a ball with mallets in the pursuit of whacking the ball into a goal. Not entirely unlike the Quidditch tournaments made popular in J.K. Rowling's *Harry Potter* series, Polo is fast-paced and requires infinite concentration as well as the abilities of any superstar athlete.

https://www.uspolo.org/

Skijoring

I did, in fact, mention this activity in the text, but I didn't provide an explanation. When executed improperly, skijoring can be a very bad idea. However, I will include a link so that you can find safe and enjoyable ways to try this Nordic sport.

http://www.skijorinternational.com/the-history

Breed Organizations

This is another area in which I will need to apologize for limiting myself. There are many horse breeds, all of which are quite amazing. The following list is simply recognition of the breeds specifically mentioned in this book, in case you wanted to learn more about each breed mentioned.

Thoroughbred: https://www.jockeyclub.com

American Quarter Horse: www.aqha.com

Lipizzaner: https://www.uslipizzan.org/

Appaloosa: https://www.appaloosa.com/

Paint Horse: https://apha.com/

Arabian: https://www.arabianhorses.org/

Hackney: http://hackneysociety.com/

Saddlebred: https://www.asha.net/

Tennessee Walker: https://twhbea.com/, https://nwha.com/

Missouri Fox Trotter: https://mfthba.com/

Icelandic: https://icelandics.org/

Morgan: https://www.morganhorse.com/

Rocky Mountain Horse: https://www.rmhorse.com/

Paso Fino: https://www.pfha.org/

DOWNLOAD YOUR FREE CHECKLIST NOW!

If you've ever checked out an equine supply website or stopped by a tack shop, you might find your head swimming regarding all of the stuff people buy to help them care for their horses. How do you decide what you need to buy? I've created this checklist to help new horse owners get organized right from the start.

Go to **https://free.meredithhillbook.com/checklist** or
scan this code

to download it for free

Reviews and feedback help improve this book and the author. If you enjoy this book, we would greatly appreciate it if you could take a few moments to share your opinion and post a review on Amazon.

LEAVE A REVIEW ON AMAZON:

https://www.amazon.com/review/create-review/listing?asin=&

ALSO BY MEREDITH HILL

Finding Your First Horse

https://www.amazon.com/dp/B09QF44ZF9

www.ingramcontent.com/pod-product-compliance
Lightning Source LLC
Chambersburg PA
CBHW061146120626
46546CB00005B/1950